THE MOUNTAIN BARD;

CONSISTING OF

Ballads and Songs,

FOUNDED ON

FACTS AND LEGENDARY TALES.

BY

JAMES HOGG,

THE ETTRICK SHEPHERD.

Fain would I hear our mountains ring
   With blasts which former minstrels blew;
Drive slumber hence on viewless wing,
   And tales of other times renew.

EDINBURGH:

Printed by J. Ballantyne and Co.
FOR ARCH. CONSTABLE AND CO. EDINBURGH,
AND JOHN MURRAY, LONDON.

1807.

TO

WALTER SCOTT, Esq.

SHERIFF OF ETTRICK FOREST,

AND

MINSTREL OF THE SCOTTISH BORDER,

THE FOLLOWING

TALES

ARE RESPECTFULLY INSCRIBED

BY HIS FRIEND AND HUMBLE SERVANT,

THE AUTHOR.

ADVERTISEMENT.

A liberal and highly respectable list of Subscribers honoured this Work with their countenance; but the circumstances of the Author, detained by the duties of his situation in a remote part of the country, has prevented the possibility of collecting their names, and prefixing them to the Book.

CONTENTS.

	PAGE.
Memoir of the Life of James Hogg,	i
Sir David Græme,	3
The Pedlar,	15
Gilmanscleuch,	35
The Fray of Elibank,	50
Mess John,	68
Death of Douglas, Lord of Liddisdale,	96
Willie Wilkin,	103
Thirlestane, a Fragment,	117
Lord Derwent,	128
The Laird of Lairistan,	137
Sandy Tod,	153
A Farewell to Ettrick,	164
Love Abused,	170
Epistle to Mr J. M. C. London,	172
Scotia's Glens,	177
Donald MacDonald,	179
The Author's Address to his auld dog Hector,	183
The Bonnets o' Bonny Dundee,	190
Auld Ettrick John,	192
The Hay Making,	197
Bonny Jean,	200

MEMOIR

OF

THE LIFE OF JAMES HOGG.

The friend, to whom Mr Hogg made the following communication, had some hesitation in committing it to the public. On the one hand, he was sensible, not only that the incidents are often trivial, but that they are narrated in a stile more suitable to their importance to the author himself, than to their own nature and consequences. But the efforts of a strong mind, and vigorous imagination, to develope itself even under the most disadvantageous circumstances, may be always considered with pleasure, and often with profit; and if, upon a retrospect, the possessor be disposed to view with self complacency his victory over difficulties, of which he only can judge the extent, it will be readily pardoned by those who consider the author's scanty opportunities of knowledge; and remember, that it is only on attaining the last, and most recondite, recess of human science, that we discover how little we really know. To those who are unacquainted with the pastoral scenes, in which our author was educated, it may afford some amusement to find real shepherds actually contending for a poetical prize, and to remark some other peculiarities in their habits and manners. Above all, these Memoirs ascertain the authenticity of the publication, and are, therefore, entitled to be prefixed to it.

Mitchell-Slack, Nov. 1806.

MY DEAR SIR,

According to your request, which I never entirely disregard, I am now going to give you some account of my manner of life and *expensive* education. I must again apprize you, that, whenever I have occasion to speak of myself, or my performances, I find it impossible to divest myself of an inherent vanity; but, making allowances for that, I will lay before you the outlines of my life, with the circumstances that gave rise to some of my juvenile pieces, and of my opinion of them, as faithfully

> As if you were the minister of heaven,
> Sent down to search the secret sins of men.

I am the second of four sons by the same father and mother, viz. Robert Hogg and Margaret Laidlaw, who, with my three brethren, are all living, and in good health. My progenitors were all shepherds of this country. My father, like myself, was bred to the occupation of a shepherd, and served in that capacity until his marriage with my mother; about which time, having saved some substance, he took a lease of the farms of Ettrickhouse and Ettrickhall. He then commenced dealing in sheep; brought up great numbers, and drove them both to the English and Scottish markets; when, at length, a great fall in the prices of sheep, and his principal debtor's absconding, quite ruined him. A sequestration* took place. Every thing was sold by auction; and my parents were turned out of doors without a farthing in the world. I was then in the sixth year of my age, and remember well the distressed and destitute condition that we were in. At length, the late worthy Mr Bryden, of Crosslee, took compassion upon us, and, taking a short lease of the farm of Ettrickhouse, placed my father there as his shepherd, and thus afforded us the means of supporting life for a time. This gentleman continued to interest himself in our welfare, until the lamented day of his untimely death, when we lost the best friend that we had in the world. It was on this mournful occasion that I wrote the *Dialogue in a Country Church-yard.*†

At such an age, it cannot be expected that I should have made great progress in knowledge. The school-house, however, being almost at our door, I had attended for some time; and had oft-times the honour of standing at the head of that juvenile class, who read the Shorter Catechism, and Proverbs of Solomon.

* *i. e.* Legal distress.
† This worthy man was killed by the fall of a tree.

At the next Whitsunday after our expulsion, I was obliged to go to service; and, being only seven years of age, was hired to a farmer in the neighbourhood to herd a few cows. Next year, my parents took me home during the winter quarter, and put me to school with a lad, who was teaching the children of a neighbouring farmer. Here I advanced so far as to get into the class who read in the Bible. I had likewise, for some time before my quarter was out, tried writing; and had horribly defiled several sheets of paper with copy-lines, every letter of which was nearly an inch in length.

Thus terminated my education:—After this I was never another day at any school whatever; and was again, that very spring, sent away to my old occupation of herding cows. This employment, the worst and lowest known in our country, I was engaged in for several years under sundry masters, till at length I got into the more honourable one of herding sheep. There is one circumstance which hath led some to imagine, that my abilities as a servant had not been exquisite; namely, that, when I was fifteen years of age, I had served a dozen of masters; which circumstance, I myself am rather willing to attribute to my having gone to service so young, that I was yearly growing stronger, and consequently adequate to a harder task, and an increase of wages: for I do not remember of ever having served a master who refused giving me a verbal recommendation to the next, especially for my inoffensive behaviour. This character, which I, some way or other, got at my very first outset, has, in some degree, attended me ever since, and has certainly been of utility to me; yet, though Solomon avers, that " a good name is rather to be chosen than great riches," I declare, that I have never been so much benefitted by mine, but that I would have chosen the latter by many degrees. From some of my masters I received very hard usage; in particular, while with one shepherd, I was often nearly exhausted by hunger and fatigue. All this while, I neither read nor wrote, nor had I access to any books, saving the Bible. I was greatly taken with our version of the Psalms of David, learned the most of them by heart, and have a great partiality for them unto this day. Every little pittance that I earned of wages, was carried directly to my parents, who supplied me with what cloaths I had. These were often scarcely worthy of the appellation; in particular, I remember of being exceedingly scarce of shirts. Time after time I had but two; which grew often so bad, that I was obliged to quit wearing them altogether; for, when I put them on, they hung down in long tatters as far as my heels. At these times I certainly made a very grotesque figure; for, on quitting the shirt, I could never induce my breeches to keep up to their proper sphere. When fourteen years of age, I saved five shillings of my wages, with which I bought an old violin. This occupied all my leisure hours, and hath been my favourite amusement ever since. I had commonly no spare time from labour during the day; but, when I was not over fatigued, I generally spent an hour or two every night in rubbing over my favourite old Scottish tunes;—my bed being always in stables and cow-houses, I disturbed nobody but myself. This brings to my remembrance an anecdote, the consequence of one of these nocturnal endeavours at improvement.

When serving with Mr Scott of Singlee, there happened to be a dance one evening, at which a number of the friends and neighbours of the family were present. I being admitted into the room as a spectator, was all attention to the music; and, on the company breaking up, I retired to my stable-loft, and fell to essaying some of the tunes to which I had been listening: the musician, going out on some necessary business, and not being aware that another of the same craft was so near him, was not a little surprised when the tones of my old violin assailed his ears. At first, he took it for the late warbles of his own ringing through his head; but, on a little attention, he, to his mortification and astonishment, perceived that the sounds were real; and that the tunes which he had lately been playing with such skill, were now murdered by some invisible being hard by him. Such a circumstance, at that dead hour of the night, and when he was unable to discern from what quarter the sounds proceeded, convinced him all at once that it was a delusion of the devil; and, suspecting his intentions from so much familiarity, he fled precipitately into the hall, with disordered garments, and in the utmost horror, to the no small mirth of Mr Scott, who declared, that he had lately been considerably stunned himself by the same discordant sounds.

From Singlee I went to Elibank upon Tweed, where, with Mr Laidlaw, I found my situation more easy and agreeable than it had ever been. I staid there three half years, a term longer than usual; and from thence went to Willenslee, to Mr Laidlaw's father, with whom I served as a shepherd two years; having been for some seasons preceding employed in working with horses, threshing, &c.

It was, while serving here, in the 18th year of my age, that I first got a perusal of "The Life and Adventures of Sir William Wallace," and "The Gentle Shepherd;" and though immoderately fond of them, yet (what you will think remarkable in one who hath since dabbled so much in verses) I could not help regretting deeply that they were not in prose, that every body might have understood them; or, I thought, if they had been in the same kind of metre with the "Psalms," I could have borne with them. The truth is, I made exceedingly slow progress in reading them: the little reading that I had learned, I had nearly lost, and the Scottish dialect quite confounded me; so that, before I got to the end of a line, I had commonly lost the rhyme of the preceding one; and if I came to a triplet, a thing of which I had no conception, I commonly read to the foot of the page without perceiving that I had lost the rhyme altogether. Thus, after I had got through them both, I found myself much in the same predicament with the man of Eskdalemuir, who borrowed Bailey's Dictionary from his neighbour. On returning it, the lender asked him, what he thought of it? "I don't know," replied he, "I have read it all through, but cannot say that I understand it; it is the most confused book that ever I saw in my life!" The late Mrs Laidlaw of Willenslee took some notice of me, and frequently gave me books to read while tending the ewes; these were chiefly theological: the only one that I remember any thing of, is *Bishop Burnet's Theory of the Conflagration of the Earth.* Happy was it for me that I did not understand it : for the little of it that I did understand, had nearly overturned my brain altogether. All the day I was pondering on the grand millenium, and the reign of the saints; and all the night dreaming of new heavens and a new earth; the stars in horror, and the world in flames! Mrs Laidlaw also gave me sometimes the newspapers, which I pored on with great earnestness; beginning at the date, and reading straight on, through advertisements of houses and lands, Balm of Gilead, and every thing; and, after all, was often no wiser than when I began. To give you some farther idea of the progress I had made in literature;—I was about this time obliged to write a letter to my elder brother, and, having never drawn a pen for such a number of years, I had actually forgot how to make sundry of the letters of the alphabet, which I had either to print, or patch up the words in the best way that I could, without them.

At Whitsunday 1790, being then in the nineteenth year of my age, I left Willenslee, and hired myself to Mr Laidlaw of Blackhouse, with whom I served as a shepherd nine years. The kindness of this gentleman to me it would be the utmost ingratitude ever to forget; for indeed it was much more like that of a father than a master; and it is not improbable that I should have been there still, had it not been for the following circumstance.

My brother William had, for some time before that, occupied the farm of Ettrick-house, where he resided with our parents; but having taken a wife, and the place not suiting two families, he took another residence, and gave up the farm to me. The lease expiring at Whitsunday 1793, our possession was taken by a wealthier neighbour. The first time that I attempted to write verses, was in the spring of the year 1793. Mr Laidlaw having a number of valuable books, which were all open to my perusal, I, about this time, began to read with considerable attention, and, no sooner did I begin to read so as to understand, than, rather prematurely, I began to write. The first thing that ever I attempted, was a poetical epistle to a student of divinity, an acquaintance of mine. It was a piece of most fulsome flattery, and was mostly composed of borrowed lines and sentences from Dryden's Virgil, and Harvey's Life of Bruce. I scarcely remember one line of it.

But the first thing that ever I composed that was really my own, was a rhyme, entitled, *An Address to the Duke of Buccleuch, in beha'f o' mysel', an' ither poor fo'k.*

In the same year, after a deal of pains, I finished a song, called, *The Way that the World goes on;* and *Wattie and Geordie' Foreign Intelligence,* an eclogue: These were my first year's productions; and having continued to write on ever since, often without either rhyme or reason, my pieces have multiplied exceedingly. Being little conversant in books, and far less in men and manners, the local circumstances on which some of my pieces are founded, may not be unentertaining to you. It was from a conversation that I had with an old woman, from Lochaber, of the name of Cameron, on which I founded the story of *Glengyle*, a ballad; and likewise the ground-plot of *The Happy Swains*, a pastoral, in four parts. This, which I suppose you have never seen, is a dramatic piece of great length, full of trifles and blunders: part of the latter were owing to my old woman, on whose word I depended, and who must have been as ignorant of the leading incidents of the year 1746 as I was.

In 1795, I began *The Scotch Gentleman*, a comedy, in five long acts; after having been summoned to Selkirk, as a witness against some persons suspected of fishing in close-time. This piece (part of which you have seen) is, in fact, full of faults; yet, on reading it to an Ettrick audience, which I have several times done, it never fails to produce the most extraordinary convulsions of laughter, besides considerable anxiety. The whole of the third act is taken up with the examination of the fishers; and many of the questions asked, and answers given in court, literally copied.* Whether my manner of writing it out was new, I know not; but it was not without singularity. Having very little spare time from my flock, which was unruly enough, I folded, and stitched a few sheets of paper, which I carried in my pocket. I had no inkhorn; but, in place of it, I borrowed a small vial, which I fixed in a hole in the breast of my waistcoat; and having a cork, affixed by a piece of twine, it answered the purpose full as well. Thus equipped, whenever a leisure minute or two offered, I had nothing ado but to sit down and write my thoughts as I found them. This is still my invariable practice in writing prose: I cannot make out one sentence by study, without the pen in my hand to catch the ideas as they arise. I seldom, or never, write two copies of the same thing.

My manner of composing poetry is very different, and, I believe, much more singular. Let the piece be of what length it will, I compose and correct it wholly in my mind, ere ever I put pen to paper, when I write it down as fast as the A B C. When once it is written, it remains in that state; it being, as you very well know, with the utmost difficulty that I can be brought to alter one line, which I think is partly owing to the above practice.

It is a fact, that, by a long acquaintance with any poetical piece, we become perfectly reconciled to its faults. The numbers, by frequently repeating, wear smoother to our minds; and the ideas having expanded, and commented by reflection on each particular scene or incident therein described, the mind cannot, without reluctance, consent to the alteration of any one part of it; for instance, how is the Scottish public likely to receive an improved edition of the Psalms of David?

My friend, Mr William Laidlaw, hath often remonstrated to me, in vain, on the necessity of a revisal of my pieces; for, in spite of him, I held fast my integrity. He was the only person who, for many years, ever pretended to discover the least merit in any of my essays, either in prose or verse; and, as he never failed to have plenty of them about him, he took the opportunity of showing them to every person, whose capacity he supposed adequate to judge of their merit; but it was all to no purpose: he could never make a proselyte to his opinion of any note, save one, who, in a little, apostatised, and left us as we were. He even went so far as to break with some of his correspondents altogether, who persisted in their obstinacy. All this had not the least effect upon me; as long as I had his applause and my own, which never failed me, I continued to persevere. He at length had the good fortune to appeal to you, who were pleased to back him, when he came off triumphant; declaring, that the world should henceforth judge for themselves for him.

I have often opposed his proposals with such obstinacy, that I was afraid of losing his countenance altogether; but none of these things had the least effect upon him; his friendship continued unimpaired, attended with the most tender assiduities for my welfare; and I am now convinced that he is better acquainted with my nature and propensities than I am myself. I have wandered insensibly from my subject; but, to return.—In the spring of the year 1796, as Alexander Laidlaw, a neighbouring shepherd, my brother William, and myself, were resting on the side of a hill above Ettrick-church, I happened, in the course of our conversation, to drop some hints of my superior talents in poetry. William said, that, as for putting words into rhyme, it was a thing which he never could do to any sense; but that if I liked to enter the lists with him in blank verse, he would take me up for any bet that I pleased. Laidlaw declared that he would venture likewise. This being settled, and the judges named, I accepted the challenge; but a dispute arising what was to be the subject, we were obliged to resort to the following mode of decision: Ten subjects were named, and lots cast, which of these was to be the topic; and, amongst them all, that which fell to be elucidated by our matchless pens, was,—*the stars!*—things which we knew little more about, than merely that they were twinkling and burning over us; to be seen every night when the clouds were away. I began with high hopes and great warmth, and in a week declared mine ready for the comparison: Laidlaw announced his next week; but my brother made us wait a full half year; and then, on being urged, presented his unfinished. The arbiters were then dispersed, and the cause was never properly judged; but those to whom they were shown, gave rather the preference to my brother's.

This is certain, that it was far superior to any of the other two in the sublimity of the ideas, but, besides being in bad measure, it is often bombastical. The title of it is, *Urania's Tour;* Laidlaw's, *Astronomical Thoughts;* and mine, *Reflections on a View of the Nocturnal Heavens.*

Alexander Laidlaw and I tried, after the same manner, a paraphrase on the 117th Psalm, in English verse. Mine is preserved in MS. I continued annually to add numbers of smaller pieces of poetry and songs to my collection, mostly on subjects purely ideal, or else adapted to the times. I had, from my childhood, been affected by the frequent return of a violent pain in my bowels, which attacked me once in a friend's house, at a distance from home, and, increasing to an inflammation, all hopes were given up of my recovery. It was while lying here, in the greatest agony, that I had the mortification of seeing the old woman, who watched with me, fall into a swoon, about the dead of the night, from a supposition that she saw my *wraith:* a spirit which the vulgar suppose to haunt the abodes of such as are instantly to die, to carry off the soul as soon as it is disengaged from the body. And, next morning, I overheard a consultation about borrowing sheets, wherein I was to be laid at my decease: but Almighty God, in his providence, deceived both them and the officious spirit; for, by the help of an able physician, I recovered, and have never since been troubled with the distemper. It was while confined to my bed from the effects of this dreadful malady that I composed the song, beginning, *Fareweel, ye Grots; fareweel, ye Glens.*

In the year 1800, I began and finished the two first acts of a tragedy, denominated, *The Castle in the Wood*; and, flattering myself that it was about to be a masterpiece, I showed it to Mr William Laidlaw, my literary confessor; who, on returning it, declared it faulty in the extreme; and perceiving that he had black strokes drawn down through several of my most elaborate speeches, I cursed his stupidity, threw it away, and never added another line. My acquaintances hereabouts imagine, that the pastoral of *Willie an' Keatie*, published with others in 1801, was founded on an amour of mine own. I cannot say that their surmises are entirely groundless. The publication of this pamphlet was one of the most unadvised actions that ever was committed.

Having attended the Edinburgh market on Monday, with a number of sheep for sale; and being unable to sell them all, I put them into a park until the market on Wednesday. Not knowing how to pass the interim, it came into my head that I would write a poem or two from my memory, and have them printed. The thought had no sooner struck me, than I put it in practice; when I was obliged to select, not the best, but those that I remembered best. I wrote as many as I could during my short stay, and gave them to a man to print at my expence; and having sold off my sheep on Wednesday morning, I returned into the Forest, and saw no more of my poems until I received word that there were one thousand copies of them thrown off. I knew no more about publishing than the man of the moon; and the only motive that influenced me was the gratification of my vanity, by seeing my works in print. But, on the first copy coming to my hand, my eyes were opened to the folly of my conduct. When I compared it with the MS. there were numbers of stanzas wanting, and others misplaced; whilst the typographical errors were without number.

Thus were my first productions pushed headlong into the world, without apprizing the public that such a thing was coming, without either patron or preface, " unhoussel'd, unanointed, unaneal'd; with all their imperfections on their heads." " Willie and Keatie," however, had the honour of being copied into some periodical publications of the time, as " no unfavourable specimen of the work," although, in my opinion, the succeeding one was greatly its superior. In 1802, *The Minstrelsy of the Scottish Border* came into my hands; and, though I was even astonished to find such exact copies of many old songs, which I had heard sung by people who never could read a song, but had them handed down by tradition; and likewise at the conformity of the notes, to the traditions and superstitions which are, even to this day, far from being eradicated from the minds of the people amongst our mountains,—yet, I confess, that I was not satisfied with many of the imitations of the ancients. I immediately chose a number of traditional facts, and set about imitating the different manners of the ancients myself. The chief of these are, *The Death of Douglas, Lord of Liddesdale, The Heir of Thirlestane, Sir David Graham, The Pedlar,* and *John Scott of Har-*

den, by the Scotts of Gilmanscleuch. The only other local circumstance on which any other of my pieces is founded, was the following :—In 1801, I went to Edinburgh on foot, and being benighted at Straiton, lodged there, where the landlord had a son deranged in his mind, whom his father described as having been formerly sensible and docile. His behaviour was very extravagant; he went out at night, and attacked the moon with great rudeness and vociferation. I was so taken with his condition, that I tarried another night on my way home, to contemplate his manner and ideas a little farther.

Thinking that a person in such a state, with a proper cause assigned, was a fit subject for a poem,—before I reached home, I had all the incidents arranged, and a good many verses composed, of the pastoral tale of *Sandy Tod*. I think it one of the best of my tender pieces. Most of my prose essays have been written in an epistolary form. You may have seen, by the papers, that I gained two premiums from the Highland Society, for essays connected with the rearing and management of sheep. I have gone three journies into the Highlands; two on foot, and one on horseback; at each time penetrating farther, until I have seen a great part of that rough, but valuable country. I have copied out the most of my journals into letters for your perusal, and will proceed with the rest at my leisure: who knows but you may one day think of laying them before the public? I have always had a great partiality for the Highlands of Scotland, and now intend going to settle in one of its most distant corners. The issue of such an adventure, time only can reveal.

———

THE above is the substance of three letters, written at the same date; since which time I have experienced a very unexpected reverse of fortune.—After our return from the Highlands, in June last, I put every thing in readiness for our departure to settle in Harries; wrote, and published, my *Fareweel to Ettrick*; wherein the real sentiments of my heart, at that time, are simply related; which, probably, constitute its only claim to merit. It would be tedious and trifling, were I to relate all the disagreeable circumstances which ensued; suffice it to say, that my scheme was absolutely frustrated.

Being miserably disappointed, and vexed at being thus baffled in an undertaking, about which I had talked so much,—to avoid a great many disagreeable questions and explanations, I went to England during the remainder of summer. This transaction did not savour with my countrymen; they looked on me as a fugitive, and railed at me without mercy; though why, or for what reason, I have never been able to comprehend, as the only person who had even the least prospect of losing by it, always stood my firm friend. It, however, gave me the opportunity of learning exactly who were really my friends; a knowledge which is of greater consequence than many are aware.

I am, &c.

JAMES HOGG.

BALLADS,

IN

IMITATION OF THE ANTIENTS.

SIR DAVID GRÆME.

Any person who has read the *Minstrelsy of the Scottish Border* with attention, must have observed what a singular degree of interest and feeling the simple ballad of " The Twa Corbies" impresses upon the mind, which is rather increased than diminished by the unfinished state in which the story is left. It appears as if the bard had found his powers of description inadequate to a detail of the circumstances attending the fatal catastrophe, without suffering the interest, already roused, to subside, and had artfully consigned it over to the fancy of every reader to paint it what way he chose; or else that he lamented the untimely fate of a knight, whose base treatment he durst not otherwise make known than in that short parabolical dialogue. That the original is not improved in the following ballad, will too manifestly appear upon perusal; I think it, however, but just to acknowledge, that the idea was suggested to me by reading " The Twa Corbies."

SIR DAVID GRÆME.

The dow flew east, the dow flew west,
   The dow flew far ayont the fell,
An' sair at e'en she seem'd distrest,
   But what perplext her could not tell.

But ay she cry'd, Cur-dow, cur-dow,
   An' ruffled a' her feathers fair;
An' lookit sad, an' wadna bow
   To taste the sweetest, finest ware.

The lady pined, an' some did blame,
   (She didna blame the bonny dow)
But sair she blamed Sir David Græme,
   Wha now to her had broke his vow.

He swore by moon and stars sae bright,
    And by their bed—the grass sae green,
To meet her there on Lammas night,
    Whatever dangers lay between:

To risk his fortune and his life,
    To bear her from her father's ha',
To give her a' the lands o' Dryfe,
    An' wed wi' her for gūde an' a'.

The day arrived, the evening came,
    The lady looked wi' wistful ee;
But, O, alas! her noble Græme
    Frae e'en to morn she could not see.

An' ilka day she sat an' grat,
    An' ilka night her fancy wraught,
In wyting this, and blaming that,
    But O the cause she never thought.

The sun had drank frae Keilder fells
    His beverage o' the morning dew;
The wild-fowl slumbered in the dells,
    The heather hung its bells o' blue;

The lambs were skipping on the brae,
   In airy notes the shepherd sung,
The small birds hailed the jocund day,
   Till ilka thicket sweetly rung.

The lady to her window hied,
   That opened owr the banks o' Tyne,
" An' O, alas !" she said, and sighed,
   " Sure ilka breast is blyth but mine !

" Where ha'e ye been, my bonny dow,
   That I ha'e fed wi' bread and wine ?
As roving a' the country through,
   O saw ye this fause knight o' mine ?"

The dow sat on the window tree,
   An' held a lock o' yellow hair;
She perched upon that lady's knee,
   An' carefully she placed it there.

" What can this mean ? it is the same,
   Or else my senses me beguile !
This lock belonged to David Græme,
   The flower of a' the British isle.

" It is not cut wi' sheers nor knife,
  But frae his haffat torn awa :
I ken he lo'ed me as his life,
  But this I canna read at a."

The dow flew east, the dow flew west,
  The dow flew far ayont the fell,
And back she came, wi' panting breast,
  Ere ringing of the castle bell.

She lighted on the hollow tap,
  An' cried, Cur-dow, an' hung her wing;
Then flew into that lady's lap,
  An' there she placed a diamond ring.

" What can this mean? it is the same,
  Or else my senses me beguile!
This ring I gave to David Græme,
  The flower of a' the British isle.

" He sends me back the tokens true!
  Was ever maid perplexed like me?
'Twould seem h'as rued o' ilka vow,
  But all is wrapt in mystery."

Then down she sat, an' sair she grat;
  With rapid whirl her fancy wrought,
In wyting this, an' blamin' that;
  But O the cause she never thought!

When, lo! Sir David's trusty hound,
  Wi' humpling back, an' hollow ee,
Came cringing in; an' lookit round
  Wi' hopeless stare, wha there might be.

He laid his head upon her knee,
  With looks that did her heart assail;
An' a' that she cou'd flatter, he
  Wad neither bark, nor wag his tail!

She fed him wi' the milk sae sweet,
  An' ilka thing that he wad ha'e.
He licked her hands, he licked her feet,
  Then slowly, slowly, trudged away.

But she has eyed the honest hound,
  An' a' to see where he wad gae:
He stopped, and howled, an' looked around,
  Then slowly, slowly, trudged away.

Then she cast aff her coal-black shoon,
    An' sae has she her silken hose;
She kiltit high her 'broidered gown,
    An' after him in haste she goes.

She followed him owr muirs and rocks,
    Through mony a dell, an' dowy glen,
Till frae her brow, and lovely locks,
    The dew-drops fell like drops o' rain.

An' ay she said, "My love is hid,
    And dare na come the castle nigh;
But him I'll find, an' him I'll chide,
    For leaving his poor maid to sigh;

"But ae press to his manly breast,
    An' ae kiss o' his bonny mou',
Will weel atone for a' the past,
    An' a' the pain I suffer now."

But in a hagg in yonder flow,
    Ah, there she fand her gallant knight!
A loathsome carcase lying low,
    Red-rusted all his armour bright:

Wi' ae wound through his shoulder-bane,
 An' in his bosom twa or three;
Wi' flies an' vermine sair o'ergane,
 An' ugsome to the sight was he.

His piercing een, that love did beet,
 Had now become the ravens' prey;
His tongue, that moved to accents sweet,
 Deep frae his throat was torn away.

Poor Reyno fawned, an' took his place,
 As glad to see the livid clay;
Then licked his master's bloated face,
 An' kindly down beside him lay.—

* * *

" Now coming was the night sae dark,
 An' gane was a' the light o' day,"
The muir was dun, the heavens mirk,
 An' deep an' dreary was the way.

The croaking raven soared on high,
　　Thick, thick, the cherking weazels ran;
At hand she heard the howlet's cry,
　　An' groans as of a dying man.

Wi' horror, an' wi' dread aghast,
　　That lady turned, an' thought o' hame;
An' there she saw, approaching fast,
　　The likeness o' her noble Græme!

His grim, grim eyelids didna move;
　　His thin, thin cheek was deadly pale;
His mouth was black, and sair he strove
　　T' impart to her some dreadfu' tale.

For thrice his withered hand he waved,
　　An' laid it on his bleedin' breast.—
Hast thou a tender heart received?
　　How thou wilt tremble at the rest!

Fain wad I tell what there befel,
　　But its unmeet for mortal ear:
The dismal deeds on yonder fell
　　Wad shock a human heart to hear.

NOTES

ON

SIR DAVID GRÆME.

The dow flew east, the dow flew west.—P. 5. v. 1.

I borrowed the above line from a beautiful old rhyme which I have often heard my mother repeat, but of which she knew no tradition; and from this introduction the part of the dove naturally arose. The rhyme runs thus:

> The heron flew east, the heron flew west,
> The heron flew to the fair forest;
> She flew o'er streams and meadows green,
> And a' to see what could be seen:
> And when she saw the faithful pair,
> Her breast grew sick, her head grew sair;
> For there she saw a lovely bower,
> Was a' clad o'er wi' lilly-flower;
> And in the bower there was a bed
> With silken sheets, and weel down spread;

And in the bed there lay a knight,
Whose wounds did bleed both day and night;
And by the bed there stood a stane,
And there was set a leal maiden,
With silver needle and silken thread,
Stemming the wounds when they did bleed.—

To gi'e her a' the lands o' Dryfe.—P. 6. v. 2.

The river Dryfe forms the south-east district of Annandale; on its banks the ruins of the tower of Græme still remain in considerable uniformity.

The sun had drunk from Keilder fells
 His beverage of the morning dew.—P. 6. v. 5.

Keilder Fells are those hills which lie eastward of the sources of North Tyne.

When, lo! Sir David's trusty hound,
 With humpling back, and hallow ee.—P. 9. v. 2.

It is not long ago since a shepherd's dog watched his corpse in the snow amongst the mountains of this country, until nearly famished, and at last led to the discovery of the body of his disfigured master.

THE

PEDLAR.

This Ballad is founded on a fact, which has been magnified by popular credulity and superstition into the terrible story which follows. It is here related, according to the best informed old people about Ettrick, as nearly as is consistent with the method pursued in telling it. I need not inform the reader, that every part of it is believed by them to be absolute truth.

'Twas late, late, late on a Saturday's night,
   The moon was set, an' the wind was lown;
The lazy mist crept toward the height,
   An' the dim, livid flame glimmered laigh on the downe.

O'er the rank-scented fen the bittern was warping,
    High on the black muir the foxes did howl,
All on the lone hearth the cricket sat harping,
    An' far on the air cam the notes o' the owl.

When the lady o' Thirlestane rose in her sleep,
    An' she shrieked sae loud that her maid ran to see;
Her e'en they war set, an' her voice it was deep,
    An' she shook like the leaf o' the aspin tree.

" O where is the pedlar I drave frae the ha',
    That pled sae sair to tarry wi' me?"
" He's gane to the mill, for the miller sells ale,
    An' the pedlar's as weel as a man can be."

" I wish he had staid, he sae earnestly prayed,
    And he hight a braw pearling in present to gie;
But I was sae hard, that I would na regard,
    Tho' I saw the saut tear trickle down frae his ee.

" But O what a terrible dream I ha'e seen,
    The pedlar a' mangled—most shocking to see!
An' he gapit, an' waggit, an' stared wi' his een,
    An' he seemed to lay a' the blame upo' me!

" I fear that alive he will never be seen,
   An' the vera suspicion o't terrifies me:
I wadna hae sickan a vision again
   For a' the guid kye upon Thirlestane lee.

" Yet wha wad presume the poor pedlar to kill?
   O, Grizzy, my girl, will ye gang and see?
If the pedlar is safe, an' alive at the mill,
   A merk o' guid money I'll gie unto thee."

" O lady, 'tis dark, and I heard the dead bell!
   And I darna gae yonder for goud nor fee:
But the miller has lodgings might serve yoursel,
   An' the pedlar's as weel as a pedlar can be."

She sat till day, and she sent wi' fear,—
   The miller said there he never had been;
She went to the kirk, and speered for him there,
   But the pedlar in life was never mair seen.

Frae aisle to aisle she lookit wi' care;
   Frae pew to pew she hurried her een;
An' a' to see if the pedlar was there,
   But the pedlar in life was never mair seen.

But late, late, late on a Saturday's night,
    As the laird was walking along the lee,
A silly auld pedlar cam bye on his right,
    An' a muckle green pack on his shoulders had he.

" O whar are ye gaeing, ye beggarly lown?
    Ye's nauther get lodging nor fall frae me."
He turned him about, an' the blude it ran down,
    An' his throat was a' hackered, an' ghastly was he.

Then straight, wi' a sound, he sank i' the ground,
    A knock was heard, an' the fire did flee;
To try a bit prayer the laird clapped down,
    As flat an' as feared as a body cude be.

He fainted:—but soon as he gathered his breath,
    He tauld what a terrible sight he had seen:
The devil a' woundit, an' bleedin to death,
    In shape o' a pedlar upo the mill-green.

The lady she shriekit, the door it was steekit,
    The servants war glad that the devil was gane;
But ilk Saturday's night, when faded the light,
    Near the mill-house the poor bleeding pedlar was seen.

An' ay whan passengers bye war gaun,
   A doolfu' voice cam frae the mill-ee,
On Saturday's night when the clock struck one,
   Cry'n, " O Rob Riddle, ha'e mercy on me!"

The place was harrassed, the mill was laid waste,
   The miller he fled to a far countrie;
But ay at e'en the pedlar was seen,
   An' at midnight the voice cam frae the mill-ee.

The lady frae hame wad never mair budge,
   From the time that the sun gaed over the hill;
An' now she had a' the poor bodies to lodge,
   As nane durst gae on for the ghost o' the mill.

But the minister there was a bodie o' skill,
   Nae feared for devil or spirit was he;
An' he's gane awa to watch at the mill,
   To try if this impudent ghaist he cou'd see.

He prayed an' he read, an' he sent them to bed;
   Then the bible anunder his arm took he,
An' round an' round the mill-house he gaed,
   To try if this terrible sight he cou'd see.

Wi' a shivering groan the pedlar cam on,
    An' the muckle green pack on his shoulders had he;
But he nouther had flesh, blude, nor bone,
    For the moon shone throw his thin bodye.

The ducks they whackit, the dogs they howled,
    The herons thy shriekit most piteouslie;
The horses they snorkit for miles around,
    While the priest an' the pedlar together might be.

Wi' a positive look he opened his book,
    An' charged him by a' the sacred Three,
To tell why that horrible figure he took,
    To terrify a' the hale countrie?

" My body was butchered within that mill,
    My banes lie under the inner mill-wheel;
An' here my spirit maun wander, until
    Some crimes an' villanies I can reveal:

" I robbed my niece of three hundred pounds,
    Which providence suffered me ne'er to enjoy;
For the sake of that money I gat my death's wounds;
    The miller me kend, but he missed his ploy.

" The money lies buried on Balderstone hill,
    Beneath the mid bourack o' three times three.
O gi'e't to the owners, kind sir, an' it will
    Bring wonderful comfort an' rest unto me.

" 'Tis drawing to day, nae mair I can say;
    My message I trust, good father, with thee.
If the black cock should craw, while I am awa,
    O, weary, and weary, what wad come o' me!"

Wi' a sound like a horn, away he was borne;
    The grass was decayed where the spirit had been:
An' certain it is, from that day to this,
    The ghost o' the pedlar was never mair seen.

The mill was repaired, and, low in the yird,
    The banes lay under the inner mill-wheel;
The box an' the ellwand beside him war hid,
    An' mony a thimble an' mony a seal.

Must the scene of iniquity cursed remain?
    Can this bear the stamp of the heavenly seal?
Yet certain it is from that day to this,
    The millers of Thirlestane ne'er ha'e done weel.

But there was an auld mason wha wrought at the mill,
    In rules o' providence skilfu' was he;
He keepit a bane o' the pedlar's heel,
    An' a queerer wee bane you never did see.

The miller had fled to the forest o' Jed;
    But time had now grizzled his haffets wi' snaw;
He was crookit an' auld, an' his head was turned bald,
    Yet his joke he cou'd brik wi' the best o' them a'.

Away to the border the mason he ran,
    To try wi' the bane if the miller was fey;
An' into a smiddie, wi' mony a man,
    He fand him a gaffin fu' gaily that day.

The mason he crackit, the mason he taukit,
    Of a' curiosities mighty an' mean;
Then pu'd out the bane, an' declared there were nane
    Who in Britain had ever the marrow o't seen.

When ilka ane took it, an' ilka ane lookit,
    An' ilka ane ca'd it a comical bane;
To the miller it goes, wha, wi' spects on his nose,
    To ha'e an' to view it, was wonderous fain.

But what was his horror, as leaning he stood,
    An' what the surprise o' the people around,
When the little wee bane fell a streamin wi' blood,
    Which dyed a' his fingers, an' ran to the ground!

They charged him wi' murder, an' a' the hale crew
    Declared, ere they partit, the hale they wad ken;
A red goad o' ern frae the fire they drew,
    An' they swore they wad spit him like ony muirhen.

" O hald," said the mason, " for how can it be?
    " You'll find you are out when the truth I reveal;
At fair Thirlestane I gat the wee bane,
    Deep buried anunder the inner mill-wheel."

" O God," said the wretch, wi' the tear in his ee,
    " O pity a creature lang doomed to despair;
A silly auld pedlar, wha begged of me
    For mercy, I murdered, an' buried him there!"

To Jeddart they hauled the auld miller wi' speed,
    An' they hangit him dead on a high gallow tree;
An' *afterwards* they in full counsel agreed,
    That Rob Riddle he richly deserved to dee.

The thief may escape the lash an' the rape,
   The liar an' swearer their leather may save,
The wrecker of unity pass with impunity,
   But when gat the murd'rer in peace to the grave?

Ca't not superstition; wi' reason you'll find it,
   Nor laugh at a story attestit sae weel;
For lang ha'e the *facts* in the forest been mindit
   O' the ghaist an' the bane o' the pedlar's heel.

NOTES

ON

THE PEDLAR.

───────

When the lady o' Thirlestane rose in her sleep.
                                            P. 16. v. 2.

The lady here alluded to was the second wife of Sir Robert Scott, the last knight of Thirlestane, of whom the reader shall hear further. Thirlestane is situated high on the banks of the Ettrick, and was the baronial castle of the Scotts of Thirlestane. It is now the property of the Right Honourable Lord Napier, who wears the arms of that ancient house. The mill is still on the old scite.

O lady, 'tis dark, and I heard the dead bell!
And I darna gae yonder for goud nor fee.
                                            P. 17. v. 3.

By the dead bell is meant a tinkling in the ears, which our peasantry in the country regard as a secret intelligence of some friend's decease. Thus this natural occurrence strikes many with a superstitious awe. This reminds me of a trifling anecdote, which I will here relate as an instance. Our two servant girls agreed to go an errand of their own, one night after supper, to a considerable distance, from which I strove to dissuade them, but could not prevail. So, after going to the apartment where I slept, I took a drinking glass, and, coming close to the back of the door, made two or three sweeps round the lips of the glass with my finger, which caused a loud shrill sound. I then overheard the following dialogue.—B. Ah, mercy! the dead bell went through my head just now, with such a knell as I never heard.—J. I heard it too!—B. Did you indeed! that is remarkable! I never knew of two hearing it at the same time before.—J. We will not go to Midgehope to-night.—B. I would not go for all the world; I shall warrant it is my poor brother Wat; who knows what these wild Irish may have done to him!

Amongst people less conversant in the manners of the cottage than I have been, it may reasonably be suspected that I am prone to magnify these vulgar superstitions, in order to give countenance to several of them hinted at in the ballads. Therefore, as this book is designed solely for amusement, I hope I shall be excused for here detailing a few more of them, which still linger amongst the wilds of the country to this day, and which I have been an eye witness to a thousand times; and from these the reader may judge what they must have been in the times to which these ballads refer.

In addition to the dead bell;—if one of the ears is at any time seized with a glowing heat, which may very easily happen, if exposed to a good fire, or a strong wind, they straight conclude that some person is talking of them. They then turn to such as are near them, and put the following question;—*Right lug, left lug, whilk lug glows?* That person immediately guesseth; and if it hit upon the one that glows, they say, " You love me better than they who talk of me;" and so conclude they are ill spoken of; but if the guesser hits upon the wrong *lug*, they say, " You love me worse than those that talk of me:" and rest satisfied that some person is saying good of them. When the nostrils itch, they are sure to hear tell of some person being dead; and the *death watch*, the *death tap*, and the *death swap*, which is a loud, sharp stroke, are still current; whilst the belief in wraiths, ghaists, and bogles, is little or nothing abated.

When they sneeze, on first stepping out of bed in the morning, they are from thence certified that strangers will be there in the course of the day, in number corresponding to the times which they sneeze; and if a feather, a straw, or any such thing, be observed hanging at a dog's nose, or beard, they call that *a guest*, and are sure of the approach of a stranger. If it hang long at the dog's nose, the visitant is to stay long; but if it falls instantly away, the person is only to stay a short time. They judge also, from the length of this *guest*, what will be the size of the real one, and, from its shape, whether it will be a man or a woman; and they watch carefully on what part of the floor it drops, as it is on that very spot the stranger will sit. And there is scarcely a shepherd in the whole country, who, if he gets one of his flock dead on the sabbath, is not from thence certified that he will have two or three more in the course of the week. During the season that the ewes are milked, the bught door is always carefully shut at even; and the reason they assign for this is, that when it is negligently left open, the witches and fairies never miss the opportunity of dancing in it all the night. Nothing in the world can be more unnatural than this supposition; for the bught is commonly so foul, that they are obliged to wade to the ancles in mud, consequently the witches could not find a more inconvenient spot for dancing, on the whole farm. Many, however, still adhere to that custom; and I was once present when an old shoe was found in the bught that none of them would claim, and they gravely and rationally concluded that one of the witches had lost it, while dancing in the night. When any of them eat an egg, as soon as they have emptied it of its contents, they always crush the shell. An English gentleman asked Mr William Laidlaw, why the Scots did that? He, being well acquainted with the old adage, replied, " That it was for fear the witches got them to sail over to Flanders in."—" What though they should," said he, " are you so much afraid that the witches leave you ?"

Whether it proceeds from a certain habit of body in the cattle, from their food, or what is the fundamental cause of it, I cannot tell; but the milk of whole herds of cows is liable at times to a strange infection, whereby it is converted into a tough jelly as soon as it cools from the udder, and is thus rendered loathsome and unfit for use. This being a great loss and grievance to the owner, it will scarcely be believed, that there are very many of the families in Ettrick and its vicinity, and some most respectable ones, who have, at some period in the present age, been driven to use very gross incantations for the removal of this from their cattle, which they believe to proceed from witchcraft. The effects of these are so apparent on the milk in future, and so well attested, that the circumstance is of itself sufficient to stagger the resolution of the most obstinate misbeliever in witchcraft, if not finally to convert him. I am not so thoroughly initiated into this mystery as to describe it minutely; but, in the first place, a fire is set on, and surrounded with green turfs, in which a great number of pins are stuck. A certain portion of the milk of each cow, so infected, is then hung on in a pot, with a horse'-shoe, and a black dish, with its mouth downward, placed in it. The doors are then carefully shut, and the milk continues to boil; and the first person that comes to that house afterwards, is always blamed for the mischief. But the poor old women are generally suspected. There are, besides, a number of other remarks, too tedious, and too common, to be minutely described here: such as, spilling salt on the ground, or milk in the fire; suffering the dish-water to boil, without putting a peat in it; shavings at candles; thirteen in a company, &c.; all which are ominous, or productive of their particular effects. Many are apt to despise their poor illiterate countrymen for these weak and superstitious notions; but I am still of opinion, that, in the circumstance of their attaching credit to them, there is as much to praise as to blame. Let it be considered, that their means of information have not been adequate to the removal of these; while, on the other hand, they have been used to hear them related, and attested as truths, by the very persons whom they were bound, by all the laws of nature and gratitude, to reverence and believe.

An' ay whan passengers bye war gaun,
A doolfu' voice cam frae the mill-ee
On Saturday's night, when the clock struck one,
Cry'ng, " O Rob Riddle, ha'e mercy on me."
P. 19. v. 1.

In addition to this cry of despair, which was sometimes heard from the mill, it was common for the ghost to go down to the side of the mill-dam at a certain hour of the night, calling out, " Ho, Rob Riddle, come home to your supper, your sowens are cold!" To account for this, tradition adds, that the miller confessed, at his death, that the pedlar came down to the mill to inform him that it was wearing late, and that he must come home to his supper, and that he took that opportunity to murder him. At other times it was heard crying, in a lamentable voice, " O saw ye ought of John Waters? Nobody has seen John Waters!" This, it seems, was the pedlar's name.

The place was harassed, the mill was laid waste.
P. 19. v. 2.

To such a height did the horror of this apparition arrive in Ettrick, that it is certain there were few in the parish who durst go to, or by the mill, after sun-set; but, unlike many of the country bogles, who assume a variety of fantastical shapes, this never appeared otherwise than in the shape of a pedlar, with a green pack on his back: and so simple and natural was his whole deportment, that few ever suspected him for the spirit, until he vanished away. He once came so near two men in the twilight, that they familiarly offered him snuff, when he instantly sunk into the earth, and left his companions in a state of insensibility.

But the minister there was a bodie o' skill,
Nue feared for devil or spirit was he.
P. 19. v. 4.

The great and worthy Mr Boston was the person who is said to have laid this ghost; and the people of Ettrick are much disappointed at finding no mention made of it in his memoirs; but some, yet alive, have heard John Corry, who was his servant, tell the following story :—One Saturday afternoon, Mr Boston came to him, and says, " John, you must rise early on Monday, and get a kilnful of oats dried before day."—" You know very well, master," said John, " that I dare not for my breath go to the mill before day."—" John," said he, " I tell you to go, and I will answer for it, that nothing shall molest you." John, who revered his master, went away, determined to obey; but that very night, said John, he went to the mill, prayed with the family, and staid very late, but charged them not to mention it. On Monday morning, John arose at two o'clock, took a horse, and went to the mill, which is scarcely a mile below the kirk; and, about a bow-shot west of the mill, Mr Boston came running by him, buttoned in his great coat, but was so wrapt in thought, that he neither perceived his servant nor his horse. When he came home at even, Mr Boston says to him, " Well, John, have you seen the pedlar?"—" No, no, sir," said John, " there was nothing troubled me; but I saw that you were yonder before me this morning."—" I did not know that you saw me," said he, " John, nor did I wish to be seen; therefore, say nothing of it." This was in March, and in May following the mill was repaired, when the remains of the pedlar and his pack were actually found, and the hearts of the poor people set at ease: for it is a received opinion, that, if the body, or bones, or any part of a murdered person is found, the ghost is then at rest, and that it leaves mankind to find out the rest. I shall only mention another instance of this: There is a place below Yarrow Kirk, called Bell's Lakes, which was for a great number of years the terror of the whole neighbourhood, from a supposition that it was haunted by a ghost: I believe the *Bogle of Bell's Lakes* has been heard of through a great part of the south of Scotland. It happened at length, that a man and his wife were casting peats at Craighope-head, a full mile from the lakes; and coming to a loose place in the morass, his spade slipped lightly down, and stuck fast in something below; but judge of their surprise, when, on pulling it out, a man's head stuck on it, with long auburn hair, and so fresh that every feature was distinguishable. This happened in the author's remembrance; and it was supposed that it was the head of one Adam Hyslop, who had evanished about forty years before, and was always supposed to have left the country; since that discovery, however, Bell's Lakes has been as free of bogles as any other place.

He prayed, an' he read, an' he sent them to bed;
Then the bible anunder his arm took he,
An' round an' round the mill-house he gaed,
To try if this terrible sight he could see.

P. 19. v. 5.

A similar story to this of Mr Boston and the pedlar, is told of a contemporary of his, the Reverend Henry Davieson, of Gallashiels.—The ghost of an old wicked laird of Buckholm, in that parish, who had died a long time previous to that period, so haunted and harassed the house, that they could not get a servant to stay about it. Whereupon, in compliance with the earnest intreaties of the family, Mr Davieson went up one night to speak to and rebuke it. After supper, he prayed with the family, and then charged them all, as they valued their peace, to go quietly to their beds. This injunction they all obeyed; but one lady lay down without undressing, and, from a small aperture in the partition, which separated her chamber from the apartment in which he was left, watched all his motions. She said, that he searched long in the bible, and folded down leaves at certain places. He then kneeled, and prayed; and afterwards taking the bible, and putting his fingers in at the places he had marked, he took it below his arm, and went out; that, prompted by curiosity, she followed him, unperceived, through several of the haunted lanes; that she sometimes heard him muttering, but saw nothing. When he came to his chamber, he acted the same scene over again, and she followed him at a distance round all the town as before. That when he came to his chamber the third time, he prayed with greater fervency than ever; and when he rose, and took the bible to go out, his looks were so stern and severe, that she was awed at the very sight of them; and, on following him out of the court-yard, she was seized with an involuntary terror, and fled back to her apartment. When the family assembled next morning to prayers, he conjured them to tell him who of them were out of bed last night; and, the rest all denying, the lady confessed the whole. " I knew," said he, " there was somebody watching me, at which I was troubled; but it was lucky for you that you did not follow me the third time; for, had you seen what I saw, you had never been yourself again: but you may now safely go out and in, up stairs and down stairs, at all hours of the night, for you will never more be troubled with Old Buckholm." Whether these traditions have taken their origin from a much earlier period, and have, by later generations, been brought down and ascribed to these well known characters; or, whether these worthy men, in commiseration of the ideal sufferings of their visionary parishioners, have really condescended to these sham watchings, it is not now easy to determine. But an age, singular as that was for devotion, would readily be as much so for superstition; for, even to this day, the country people, who have the deepest sense of religion, are always those who believe most firmly in supernatural agency.

Yet certain it is, from that day to this,
  The millers of Thirlestane ne'er have done weel.
                                            P. 21. v. 5.

Though a pretext can scarcely be found in the annals of superstition sufficient to authorise the ascribing of this to the murder of the pedlar, so many ages before, yet the misfortunes attending the millers of Thirlstane are so obvious, as to have become proverbial: and when any of the neighbours occasionally mention this, along with it the murder of the pedlar is always hinted at. And it is scarcely thirty years since one of the millers was tried for his life for scoring a woman whom he supposed a witch. He had long suspected her as the cause of all the misfortunes attending him, and, enticing her into the kiln one Sabbath evening, he seized her forcibly, and cut the shape of the cross on her forehead: This they call, *scoring aboon the breath*, which overthrows their power of doing them any further mischief.

And afterwards *they in full council agreed,*
  That Rob Riddle he rickly deserved to dee.
                                               P. 23. v. 5.

This alludes to an old and very common proverb, "That such a one will get Jeddart justice:" which is, first to hang a man, and then judge whether he was guilty or not.

GILMANSCLEUCH.

FOUNDED UPON AN ANCIENT FAMILY TRADITION.

" Whair ha'e ye laid the goud, Peggye,
   Ye gat on New-Yeir's day?
I lookit ilka day to see
   Ye drest in fine array;

" But nouther kirtle, cap, nor gowne,
   To Peggye has come hame;
Whair ha'e ye stowed the gowde, dochter?
   I feir ye have been to blame."

" My goud it was my ain, father;
   A gift is ever free;
And when I neid my goud agene,
   Can it be tint to me?"

" O ha'e ye sent it to a friend?
  Or lent it to a fae?
 Or gi'en it to some fause leman,
  To breid ye mickle wae?"

" I ha'e na' sent it to a friend,
  Nor lent it to a fae,
 And never man, without your ken,
  Sal cause my joye or wae;

" I ga'e it to a poor auld man,
  Came shivering to the dore;
 And when I heard his waesome tale
  I wust my treasure more."

" What was the beggar's tale, Peggye?
  I fain wald hear it o'er;
 I fain wald hear that wylie tale
  That drained thy little store."

" His hair was like the thistle downe,
  His cheeks were furred wi' tyme,
 His beard was like a bush of lyng,
  When silvered o'er wi' ryme;

" He lifted up his languid eye,
    Whilk better days had seen;
And ay he heaved the mournfu' sye,
    While saut teirs fell atween.

" He took me by the hands, and saide,
    While pleasantly he smiled,—
O weel to you, my little flower,
    That blumes in desart wilde;

" And may ye never feel the waes
    That lang ha'e followit me;
Bereivit of all my gudes and gear,
    My friends and familye.

" In Gilmanscleuch, beneath the heuch,
    My fathers lang did dwell;
Ay formost, under bauld Buccleuch,
    A foreign fae to quell.

" Ilk petty robber, through the lands,
    They taucht to stand in awe;
And affen checked the plundrin' bands
    Of famous Tushilaw.

" But when the bush was in the flush,
 And fairer there was nane,
Ae blast did all its honours crush,
 And Gilmanscleuch is gane!

" I had ane brither, stout and trew,
 But furious, fierce, and keen;
Ane only sister, sweet and young,
 Her name was luvly Jean.

" Hir hair was like the threads of goud,
 Hir cheeks of rosy hew,
Hir eyne war like the huntin' hawks
 That owr the cassel flew.

" Of fairest fashion was hir form,
 Hir skin the driven snaw,
That's drifted by the wintery storm
 On lofty Gilman's-law.

" Hir face a smile perpetual wore,
 Her teeth were ivorie,
Hir lips the little purple floure
 That blumes on Baillie-lee.

"But, mark! what dool and care, fair maid,
 For beauty's but a snare,
Young Jock of Harden her betrayed,
 Whilk greeved us wonder sair.

"My brother Adam stormed and raged,
 And swore in aungry mood,
Either to right his dear sister,
 Or shed the traytor's blood.

"I kend his honor fair and firm,
 And didna doubt his faithe,
But being youngest of seven brethren,
 To marry he was laith.

"When June had decked the braes in grene,
 And flushed the forest tree;
When young deers ranne on ilka hill,
 And lambs on ilka lee;

"A shepherd frae our mountains hied,
 Ane ill death mot he dee!
' O master, master, haste,' he cried,
 ' O haste alang wi' me?

' Our ewes are banished frae the glen,
  Their lambs ar drawn away,
 The fairest raes on Eldin braes
  Ar Jock of Harden's prey.

' His hounds are ringing through your woods,
  And manye deer ar slaine;
 A herd is fled to Douglas-Craig,
  Will ne'er return againe.

' Your brother Adam, stout and strong,
  I warned on yon hill-side;
 And he's awa to Yarrow's banks,
  As fast as hee can ride.'

" O ill betide thy haste, young man!
  Thou micht ha'e tald it me;
 Thou kend, to hunt on all my lande,
  The Harden lads were free.

" Gae, saddel me my milk-white steed,
  Gae, saddel him suddenly;
 To Yarrow banks I'll hie wi' speed,
  This bauld huntir to see.

" But, low, low down, on Sundhop broom,
    My brother Harden spyd;
  And, with a stern and furious look,
    He up to him did ride.—

' Was't not enough, thou traytor strong,
    My sister to betray?
  That thou shouldst scare my feebil ewes,
    And chase their lambs away?

' Thy hounds ar ringing through our woods,
    Our choizest deers ar slaine;
  And hundreds fledd to Stuart's hills,
    Wull ne'er returne againe.'

' It setts thee weel, thou haughtye youth,
    To bend such taunts on me;
  Oft ha'e you hunted Aikwood hills,
    And no man hindered thee.'

' But wilt thou wedd my dear sister?
    Now tell me—aye or nay.'
' Nae questions will I answer thee,
    That's speerit in sic a way.

' Tak this for truth, I ne'er meant ill
  To nouther thee nor thine.'
Then spurrit his steed against the hill,
  Was fleeter than the hynde.

" He set a buglet to his mouth,
  And blew baith loud and cleir;
A sign to all his merry men
  Their huntin to forbear.

' O turn thee, turn thee, trayter strong;'
  Cried Adam bitterlie;
' Nae haughtye Scott, of Harden's kin,
  Sal proodlye scool on me.

' Now draw thy sword, or gi'e thy word,
  For one of them I'll have,
Or to thy face I'll thee disgrace,
  And ca' thee coward knave.'

" He sprang frae aff his coal-black steed,
  And tied him to a wande;
Then threw his bonnet aff his head,
  And drew his deidlye brande.

" And lang they foucht, and sair they foucht,
    Wi' swords of mettyl kene,
Till clotted blud, in mony a spot,
    Was sprynkelit on the grene.

" And lang they foucht, and sair they foucht,
    For braiver there war nane;
Braive Adam's thye was baithit in blud,
    And Harden's coller bane.

" Though Adam was baith stark and gude,
    Nae langer cou'd he stande;
His hand claive to his hivvye sword,
    His nees plett lyke the wande.

" He leanit himsel agenst ane aek,
    Nae mair cou'd act his parte;
A wudman then sprang frae the brume,
    And percit young Harden's herte.

" Bein yald and stout, he wheelit about,
    And kluve his heid in twaine;
Then calmlye laide him on the grene,
    Niver to ryse againe.

"I raid owr heicht, I raid through howe,
　　And ferr outstrippit the wynde,
And sent my voyce the forest throw,
　　But naething cou'd I fynde.

" And whan I came, the dysmal syghte
　　Wad melt an herte of stane!
My brither fent and bleiden laye,
　　Young Harden neirly gane.

' And art thou there, O Gilmanscleuch!
　　Wi' faltren tongue he cried,
Hadst thou arrivit tyme eneuch,
　　Thy kinsmen hadna died.

' Be kind unto thy sister Jean,
　　Whatever may betide;
This nycht I meint, at Gilmanscleuch,
　　To maik of hir my bride:

' But this sad fraye, this fatal daye,
　　May breid baith dule and payne,
My freckle brithren ne'er will staye
　　Till they're avengit or slayne.'—

"The wudman sleeps in Sundhope-brome,
 Into a lowlye grave;
Young Jock they bure to Harden's tome,
 And layde him wi' the lave.

" Thus fell that brave and cumlye youth,
 Whose arm was like the steel;
Whose very look was opin truth,
 Whose heart was trew and leel.

" It's now full three-and-thirty zeirs
 Syn that unhappye daye,
And late I saw his cumlye corpse
 Without the leist dekaye:

" The garland cross his breast aboon,
 Still held its varied hew;
The roses bloomed upon his shoon
 As faire as if they grew.

" I raised our vassals ane and a',
 Wi' mickil care and pain,
Expecting Harden's furious sons
 Wi' all their faither's train.

" But Harden was a weirdly man,
 A cunnin tod was he;
He lockit his sons in prison straung,
 And wi' him bore the key.

" And hee's awa to Holy Rood,
 Amang our nobles a',
With bonnit lyke a girdel braid,
 And hayre like Craighop snaw;

" His coat was of the forest grene,
 Wi' buttons lyke the moon;
His breeks war of the gude buck-skynne,
 Wi' a' the hayre aboon.

" His twa-hand sword hang round his neck,
 And rattled to his heel;
The rowels of his silver spurs,
 Were of the Rippon steel;

" His hose were braced wi' chains of airn,
 And round wi' tassels hung,
At ilka tramp of Harden's heel
 The royal arches rung.

" The courtly nobles of the north
  The chief with wonder eyed,
But Harden's form, and Harden's look,
  Were hard to be denied.

" Hee made his plaint unto our king,
  And magnified the deed;
While high Buccleuch, with pith enouch,
  Made Harden better speed.

" Ane grant of all our lands sae fayre,
  The king to him has gi'en,
And all the Scotts of Gilmanscleuch
  War outlawed ilka ane.

' The time I mist, and never wist
  Of nae sic treacherye,
Till I got word frae kind Traquare,
  The country shune to flee.

" For mee and mine nae friend wad fynd,
  But fa' ane easy preye;
While yet my brither weakly was,
  And scarce could brook the way.

" Now I ha'e foucht in forreign fields,
    In mony a bluddy fray,
But langed to see my native hills
    Afore my dying day.

" My brother fell in Hungarye,
    When fighting by my side;
My luckless sister bore ane son,
    But broke hir heart and dyed.

" That son, now a' my earthly care,
    Of port and stature fine;
He has thine eye, and is thy blood,
    As weel as he is mine.

" For me, I'm but a puir auld man,
    That nane regairds ava;
The peaceful grave will end my care,
    Where I maun shortly fa'."——

" I ga'e him a' my goud, father,
    I gat on New-Year's day;
And welcomed him to Harden-ha',
    With us a while to stay."

" My sweet Peggye, my dear Peggye,
 Ye ay were dear to me;
For ilka bonnet-piece ye gave,
 My love, ye shall ha'e three.

" Auld Gilmanscleuch sal share wi' me
 The table and the ha';
We'll tell of a' our doughty deeds
 At hame and far awa.

" That youth, my hapless brother's son,
 Who bears our eye and name,
Sal farm the lands of Gilmanscleuch,
 While Harden halds the same.

" Nae rent, nor kane, nor service mean,
 I'll ask at him at a',
Only to stand at my ryht hand
 When Branxholm gi'es the ca'.

" A Scott shou'd ay support a Scott,
 When sinking to decaye,
Till over a' the southlan' hills
 We stretch our ample sway."

c

THE
FRAY OF ELIBANK.

This Ballad is likewise founded on a well known and well authenticated fact. I am only uncertain what was the name of HARDEN's *son, who was taken prisoner, and forced to marry* MURRAY's *youngest daughter; but he was either brother or nephew to him who was slain in Yarrow by the* SCOTTS *of Gilmanscleuch.*

O WHA hasna heard o' the bauld Juden Murray,
 The lord o' the Elibank castle, sae high?
An' wha hasna heard o' that terrible hurry,
 Whan Wattie o' Harden was catched wi' the kye?

Auld Harden was ever the king o' gude fellows,
   His tables were filled in the room an' the ha';
But peace on the border, that thinned his keyloes,
   And want for his lads, was the warst thing of a'.

Young Harden was bauld as the Persian lion,
   And langed his skill and his courage to try;
Stout Willie o' Fauldshope ae night he did cry on,
   Frae danger or peril wha never wad fly.

" O Willie! ye ken our retainers are mony,
   Our kye they rout thin on the loan and the lee;
A drove we maun ha'e for our pastures sae bonny,
   Or Harden's ae cow aince again we may see.

" Fain wad I, but darena, gang over the border,
   Buccleuch wad restrain us, and ruin us quite;
He's bound to keep a' the wide marches in order;
   Then where shall we gae, and we'll venture to-
      night?"

"O master! ye ken how the Murrays have grund you,
   And aften caroused on your beef and your veal;

Yet, spite o' your wiles and your spies they have
        shunned you,—
A Murray is kittler to catch than the diel!

" Rough Juden o' Eli's grown doited and silly,
    He fights wi' his women frae mornin' till e'en,
Yet three hunder gude kye has the thrifty auld billy,
    As fair sleekit keyloes as ever was seen."

" Then, Willie, this night will we herry auld Juden;
    Nae danger I fear while thy weapon I see:
That time when we vanquished the outlaw of Sowden,
    The best o' his men were mishackered by thee.

" If we had his kye in the byres of Aekwood,
    He's welcome to claim the best way he can;
But sair he'll be puzzled his title to make good,
    For a' he's a cunning and dexterous man."

Auld Juden he strayed by the side of a river,
    When the watcher on Hanginshaw-law loud did
        cry,—
" Ho, Juden, take care! or ye're ruined for ever,
    The bugle of Aekwood has thrice sounded high."

" Ha, faith!" then quo' Juden, " they're naething
    to lippen,
I wonder sae lang frae a ploy they could cease;
Gae, blaw the wee horn; gar my villains come
    trippin':
I have o'er mony kye to get rested in peace."

With that a wee fellow came puffing and blawin',
    Frae high Philip-cairn a' the gate he had run;—
" O Juden, be handy, and countna the lawin',
    But warn well, and arm well, or else ye're undone!

" Young Wattie o' Harden has crossed the Yarrow,
    Wi' mony a hardy and desperate man;
The Hoggs and the Brydens have brought him to
    dare you,
    For the Wild Boar of Fauldshop he strides in the
        van."

" God's mercy!" quo' Juden, " gae blaw the great
    bugle;
Warn Plora, Traquair, and the fierce Hollowlee.
We'll gi'e them a fleg: but I like that cursed Hogg ill,
    Nae devil in hell but I rather wad see.

" To him men in arms are the same thing as thistles;
    At Ancram and Sowden his prowess I saw;
But a bullet or arrow will suple his bristles,
    And lay him as laigh as the least o' them a'."

The kye they lay down by the side of the Weel
    On the Elibank craig and the Ashiesteel bourn;
And ere the king's elwand came over the hill,
    Afore Wat and his men rattled mony a horn.

But Juden, as cunning as Harden was strong,
    On ilka man's bonnet has placed a white feather;
And the night being dark, to the peel height they
        thrang,
    And sae closely they darned them amang the
        deep heather.

Where the brae it was steep, and the kye they did
        wend,
    And sair for their pastures forsaken they strave,
Till Willie o' Fauldshop, wi' half o' the men,
    Went aff wi' a few to encourage the lave.

Nae sooner was Willie gane o'er the height,
    Than up start the Murrays, and fiercely set on;
And sic a het fight, in the howe o' the night,
    In the forest of Ettrick has hardly been known.

Soon weapons were clashing, and fire was flashing,
    And red ran the blood down the Ashiesteel bourn;
The parties were shouting, the kye they were routing,
    Confusion did gallop, and fury did burn.

But though weapons were clashing, and the fire it
        was flashing,
    Though the wounded and dying did dismally
        groan;
Though parties were shouting, the kye they came
        routing,
    And Willie o' Fauldshop drave heedlessly on!

O Willie, O Willie, how sad the disaster!
    Had some kindly spirit but whispered your ear—
" O Willie, return, and relieve your kind master,
    Wha's fighting surrounded wi' mony a spear."

Surrounded he was; but his brave little band,
   Determined, unmoved as the mountain they stood;
In hopes that their hero was coming to hand,
   Their master they guarded in streams of their blood.

In vain was their valour, in vain was their skill,
   In vain has young Harden a multitude slain,
By numbers o'erpowered they were slaughtered at will,
   And Wattie o' Harden was prisoner ta'en.

His hands and his feet they ha'e bound like a sheep,
   And away to the Elibank tower they did hie,
And they locked him down in a dungeon sae deep,
   And they bade him prepare on the morrow to die.

Though Andrew o' Langhop had fa'n i' the fight,
   He only lay still till the battle was bye;
Then ventured to rise, and climb over the height,
   And there he set up a lamentable cry.—

"Ho, Willie o' Fauldshop! Ho, all is warected!
  Ho! what's to come o' you? or whar are ye gane?
Your friends they are slaughtered, your honour suspected,
  And Wattie o' Harden is prisoner ta'en."

Nae boar in the forest, when hunted and wounded;
  Nae lion or tiger bereaved of their prey,
Did ever sae storm, or was ever sae stounded,
  As Willie, when warned o' that desperate fray.

He threw off his jacket, wi' harnass well lined;
  He threw off his bonnet well belted wi' steel;
And off he has run, wi' his troopers behind,
  To rescue the lad that they likit sae weel.

But when they arrived on the Elibank green,
  The yett was shut, and the east grew pale;
They slinkit away, wi' the tears i' their een,
  To tell to Auld Harden their sorrowfu' tale.

Though Harden was grieved, he durst venture nae further,
  But left his poor son to submit to his fate;

"If I lose him," quo' he, "I can soon get another,
  But never again wad get sic an estate."

Some say that a stock was begun that night,
  But I canna tell whether 'tis true or a lie,
That muckle Jock Ballantyne, time of the fight,
  Made off wi' a dozen of Elibank kye.

Brave Robin o' Singly was killed i' the stoure,
  And Kirkhope, and Whitsled, and young Baileylee;
Wi' Juden, baith Gatehop and Plora fell o'er,
  And auld Ashiesteel gat a cut on the knee.

And mony a brave fellow, cut off in their bloom,
  Lie rotting in cairns on the craig and the steele;
Weep o'er them, ye shepherds, how hapless their doom!
  Their natures how faithful, undaunted and leel!

The lady o' Elibank rase wi' the dawn,
  And she wakened auld Juden, and to him did say—
"Pray, what will ye do wi' this gallant young man?"
  "We'll hang him," quo' Juden, "this very same day."

" Wad ye hang sic a brisk and a gallant young heir,
 And has three hamely daughters ay suffering ne-
  glect?
Though laird o' the best o' the Forest sae fair,
 He'll marry the warst for the sake of his neck.

" Despise not the lad for a perilous feat;
 He's a friend will bestead you, and stand by you still;
The laird maun ha'e men, and the men maun ha'e meat,
 And the meat maun be had, be the danger what
  will."

Then Juden he leugh, and he rubbit his leg,
 And he thought that the lady was perfectly right;
" By heaven," said he, " he shall marry my Meg!
 I dreamed, and I dreamed o' her a' the last night."

Now Meg was but thin, an' her nose it was lang;
 And her mou' was as muckle as muckle could be;
Her een they war grey, and her colour was wan,
 But her nature was generous, gentle, and free;

Her shape it was slender, her arms they were fine;
    Her shoulders were clad wi' her lang dusky hair;
And three times mae beauties adorned her mind,
    Then mony a ane that was three times as fair.

Poor Wat, wi' a guard, was brought into a ha',
    Where ae end was black, and the ither was fair;
There Juden's three daughters sat in a raw,
    And himsel' at the head in a twa-elbow chair:—

" Now, Wat, as ye're young, and I hope ye will mend,
    On the following conditions I grant ye your life,—
Be shifty, be warie, be auld Juden's friend,
    And accept of my daughter there, Meg, for your wife.

" And since ye're sae keen o' my Elibank kye,
    Ye's ha'e each o' your drove ye can ken by the head;
And if nae horned acquaintance should kythe to your eye,
    Ye shall wale half a score, and a bull for a breed.

" My Meg, I assure you, is better than bonny;
   I reade you in choicing, let prudence decide;
Then say whilk ye will; ye are welcome to ony:
   See, there is your coffin, or there is your bride."

" Lead on to the gallows, then," Wattie replied;
   " I'm now in your power, and ye carry it high;
Nae daughter of yours shall e'er lie by my side;
   A Scott, ye maun mind, counts it naething to die."

" Amen! then," quo' Juden, " lead on to the tree,
   Your raid ye shall rue wi' the loss of your breath.
My Meg, let me tell ye, is better than thee;
   How dare ye, sir, rob us, and lightly us baith?"

When Wat saw the tether drawn over the tree,
   His courage misga'e him, his heart it grew sair;
He watch'd Juden's face, and he watched his ee,
   But the devil a scrap of reluctance was there.

He fand the last gleam of his hope was a fadin';
   The fair face of nature nae mair he wald see.
The coffin was set, where he soon must be laid in;
   His proud heart was humbled—he fell on his knee!

" O sir, but ye're hurried! I humbly implore ye
    To grant me three days to examine my mind;
To think on my sins, and the prospect before me,
    And balance your offer of freedom sae kind."

" My friendship ye spurned; my daughter ye scorned;
    This minute in air ye shall flaff at the spauld:
A preciouser villain my tree ne'er adorned;
    Hang a rogue when he's young, he'll steal nane when he's auld."

" O sir, but 'tis hard to dash me in eternity
    Wi' as little time to consider my state."—
" I swear, then, this hour shall my daughter be married t' ye,
    Or else the next minute submit to your fate."

But Wattie now fand he was fairly warang,
    That marriage to death was a different case.—
" What matter," quo' he, " though her nose it be lang?
    It will ay keep her ae bieldy side of a face.

" To fondle, or kiss her, I'll never be fain,
   Or lie down beside her wi' nought but my sark;
But the first, if I please, I can let it alane;
   And cats they are all alike grey in the dark.

" What though she has twa little winkling een?
   They're better than nane, and my life it is sweet:
And what though her mou' be the maist I ha'e seen?
   Faith, muckle-mou'd fock ha'e a luck for their meat."

That day they were wedded, that night they were bedded,
   And Juden has feasted them gayly and free;
But aft the bridegroom has he rallied and bladded,
   What faces he made at the big hanging tree.

He swore that his mou' was grown wider than Meg's;
   That his face frae the chin was a half a yard high;
That it struck wi' a palsy his knees and his legs;
   For a' that a Scott thought it naething to die!

" There's nothing," he said, " I more highly approve
 Than a rich forest laird to come stealing my kye;
Wad Branxholm and Thirlestane come for a drove,
 I wad furnish them wives in their bosoms to lie."

So Wattie took Meg to the Forest sae fair,
 And they lived a most happy and peaceable life:
The langer he kend her, he lo'ed her the mair,
 For a prudent, a virtuous, and sensible wife.

And muckle good blood frae that union has flowed,
 And mony a brave fellow, and mony a brave feat;
I darna just say they are a' muckle mou'd,
 But they rather have a' a good luck for their meat.

NOTES

ON

THE FRAY OF ELIBANK.

O wha hasna heard o' the bauld Juden Murray,
The lord of the Elibank castle, so high?

P. 50. v. 1.

Sir Gideon Murray was ancestor of the present Lord Elibank. The ruins of his huge castle still stand on the side of a hill, overhanging the Tweed, in the shire of Selkirk. Lovel Traquair, who was then Murray, Philliphaugh, Plora, and Sundhope, were all kinsmen of his; and there is a tradition extant, that all the land betwixt Tweed and Yarrow once pertained to the potent name of Murray. If so, their possessions must have bordered a great way with Harden's. The castle of Aekwood, or Oakwood, the baronial residence of the latter, stands on the Ettrick, about eight miles south of Elibank. The other places mentioned are all in that neighbourhood.

Stout Willie of Fauldshop ae night he did cry on,
Frae danger or peril wha never wad fly.

P. 51. v. 2.

This man's name was William Hogg, better known by the epithet of *The Wild Boar of Fauldshop.* Tradition reports him as a man of unequalled strength, courage, and ferocity. He was Harden's chief champion, and in great favour with his master, until once, by his temerity, he led him into a scrape that had well nigh cost him his life. It was never positively said what this scrape was, but there is reason to suppose it was the Fray of Elibank.

The Hoggs and the Brydens have brought him to dare you.

P. 53. v. 3.

The author's progenitors possessed the lands of Fauldshop, under the Scotts of Harden, for ages; until the extravagance of John Scott occasioned the family to part with them. They now form part of the extensive estates of Buccleugh. Several of their wives were supposed to be rank witches; and it is probable that the famous witch of Fauldshop was one of them, who so terribly hectored Mr Michael Scott, by turning him into a hare, and hunting him with his own dogs, until forced to take shelter in his own jaw-hole. The cruel retaliation which he made in showing his art to her, is also well known. It appears also, that some of the Hoggs had been poets before now, as there is still a part of an old song extant relating much to them. Observe how elegantly it flows on :—

* * * * * *

And the rough Hoggs of Fauldshop,
   That wear both wool and hair;
There's nae sic Hoggs as Fauldshop's,
   In all Saint Boswell's fair.

And afterwards, near the end:—

> But the hardy Hoggs of Fauldshop,
>   For courage, blood, and bane;
> For the Wild Boar of Fauldshop,
>   Like him was never nane.
> If ye reave the Hoggs of Fauldshop,
>   Ye herry Harden's gear;
> But the poor Hoggs of Fauldshop
>   Have had a stormy year.

The Brydens, too, have long been a numerous and respectable clan in Ettrick forest and its vicinity.

So Wattie took Meg to the Forest sae fair.
P. 64. v. 2.

Though Elibank is in the shire of Selkirk, as well as Oakwood, yet, originally, by Ettrick Forest, was meant only the banks and environs of the two rivers, Ettrick and Yarrow.

MESS JOHN.

This is a very popular story about Ettrick Forest, as well as a part of Annandale and Tweeddale, and is always told with the least variation, both by young and old, of any legendary tale I ever heard. It seems, like many others, to be partly founded on facts, with a great deal of romance added; for, if tradition can be in aught believed, the murder of the priest seems well attested: but I do not know if any records mention it. His sirname is said to have been Binram, though some suppose that it was only a nickname; and the mount, under which he was buried, still retains the name of Binram's Corse. A gentleman of that country, with whom I lately conversed, strove to convince me that I had placed the era of the tale too late, for that it must have had its origin from a much earlier age. But when was there ever a more romantic, or more visionary age, than that to which this ballad refers? Besides, it is certain, that the two heroes, Dobson and Dun, whom every one allows to have been the first who had the courage to lay hold on the lady, and to have slain the priest, skulked about the head of Moffat water during the heat of the persecution, which they both survived. And Andrew Moore, who died at Ettrick about 26 years ago, at a great age, often averred, that he had, in his youth, seen and conversed with many people, who remembered every circumstance of it, both as to the murder of the priest, and the road being laid waste by the woman running at night with a fire-pan, or, as some call it, a globe of fire, on her head. This singular old man could repeat by heart every old ballad which is now published in the " Minstrelsy of the Border," except three, with three times as many; and from him, *Auld Maitland*, with many ancient songs and tales, still popular in that country, are derived.

If I may then venture a conjecture at the whole of this story, it is nowise improbable that the lass of Craigyburn was some enthusiast in religious matters, or perhaps a lunatic; and that, being troubled with a sense of guilt, and a squeamish conscience, she had, on that account, made several visits to Saint Mary's

Chapel to obtain absolution: and it is well known, that many of the Mountain-men wanted only a hair to make a tether of. Might they not then frame this whole story about the sorcery, on purpose to justify their violent procedure in the eyes of their countrymen, as no bait was more likely to be swallowed at that time? But, however it was, the reader has the story, in the following ballad, much as I have it.

MESS JOHN.

Mess John stood in St Mary's kirk,
   And preached and prayed so mightilie,
No priest nor bishop through the land,
   Could preach or pray so well as he:

The words of peace flowed from his tongue,
   His heart seemed rapt with heavenly flame,
And thousands would the chapel throng,
   So distant flew his pious fame.

His face was like the rising moon,
   Imblushed with evening's purple dye;
His stature like the graceful pine
   That grew on Bourhop hills so high.

Mess John lay on his lonely couch,
   And now he sighed and sorely pined;
A smothered flame consumed his heart,
   And tainted his capacious mind.

It was not for the nation's sin,
   Nor kirk oppressed, that he did mourn;
'Twas for a little earthly flower—
   The bonny Lass of Craigyburn.

Whene'er his eyes with her's did meet,
   They pierced his heart without remede;
And when he heard her voice so sweet,
   Mess John forgot to say his creed.

" Curse on our stubborn law," he said,
   " That chains us back from social joy;
Those sweet desires, by nature lent,
   I cannot taste without alloy!

" Give misers wealth, and monarchs power;
   Give heroes kingdoms to o'erturn;
Give sophists talents depths to scan—
   Give me the lass of Craigyburn."

Pale grew his cheek, and howe his eye,
   His holy zeal, alas! is flown;
A priest in love is like the grass,
   That fades ere it be fairly grown.

When thinking on her cherry lip,
   Her maiden bosom fair and gay,
Her limbs, the ivory polished fine,
   His heart, like wax, would melt away!

He tried the sermons to compose,
   He tried it both by night and day;
But all his lair and logic failed,
   His thoughts were ay on bonny May.

He said the creed, he sung the mass,
   And o'er the breviary did turn;
But still his wayward fancy eyed
   The bonny lass of Craigyburn.

One day, upon his lonely couch
   He lay, a prey to passion fell;
And aft he turned—and aft he wished—
   What 'tis unmeet for me to tell.

A sudden languor chilled his blood,
   And quick o'er all his senses flew;
But what it was, or what the cause,
   He neither wished to know, nor knew:

But first he heard the thunder roll,
   And then a laugh of malice keen;
Fierce whirlwinds shook the mansion-walls,
   And grievous sobs were heard between:

And then a maid, of beauty bright,
   With bosom bare, and claithing thin,
With many a wild fantastic air,
   To his bedside came gliding in.

A silken mantle on her feet
   Fell down in many a fold and turn,
He thought he saw the lovely form
   Of bonny May of Craigyburn!

Though eye and tongue and every limb
   Lay chained as the mountain rock,
Yet fast his fluttering pulses played,
   As thus the enticing demon spoke:—

" Poor heartless man! and wilt thou lie
   A prey to this devouring flame?
That thou possess not bonny May,
   None but thyself hast thou to blame.

" You little know the fervid fires
   In female breasts that burn so clear;
The forward youth of fierce desires,
   To them is most supremely dear.

" Who ventures most to gain their charms,
   By them is ever most approved;
The ardent kiss, and clasping arms,
   By them are ever best beloved.

" Then mould her form of fairest wax,
   With adder's eyes, and feet of horn:
Place this small scroll within its breast,
   Which I, your friend, have hither borne.

" Then make a blaze of alder wood,
   Before your fire make this to stand;
And the last night of every moon
   The bonny May's at your command.

"　With fire and steel to urge her weel,
　　See that you neither stint nor spare;
　For if the cock be heard to crow,
　　The charm will vanish into air."

Then bristly, bristly, grew her hair,
　Her colour changed to black and blue;
And broader, broader, grew her face,
　Till with a yell away she flew!

The charm was gone: Upstarts Mess John,
　A statue now behold him stand;
Fain, fain, he would suppose't a dream,
　But, lo, the scroll is in his hand.

Read through this tale, and, as you pass,
　You'll cry, alas, the priest's a man!
Read how he used the bonny lass,
　And count him human if you can.

" O Father dear! what ails my heart?
 Ev'n but this minute I was well;
And now, though still in health and strength,
 I suffer half the pains of hell."

" My bonny May, my darling child,
 Ill wots thy father what to say;
I fear 'tis for some secret sin
 That heaven this scourge on thee doth lay;

" Confess, and to thy Maker pray;
 He's kind; be firm, and banish fear;
He'll lay no more on my poor child,
 Than he gives strength of mind to bear."

" A thousand poignards pierce my heart!
 I feel, I feel, I must away;
Yon holy man at Mary's kirk
 Will pardon, and my pains allay.

" I mind, when, on a doleful night,
 A picture of this black despair
Was fully opened to my sight,
 A vision bade me hasten there."

" O stay, my child, till morning dawn,
 The night is dark, and danger nigh;
Yon persecuted desperate bands
 Will shoot thee for a nightly spy.

" Where wild Polmoody's mountains tower,
 Full many a wight their vigils keep:
Where roars the torrent from Loch-Skene,
 A troop is lodged in trenches deep.

" The howling fox and raving earn
 Will scare thy reason quite away;
Regard thy sex, and tender youth,
 And stay, my child, till dawning day."

" I burn!—I rage!—my heart, my heart!"
 Then, with a shriek, away she ran.
Hope says she'll lose her darkling way,
 And never reach that hated man.

But lo! a magic lanthorn bright
 Hung on the birks of Craigyburn;
She placed the wonder on her head,
 Which shone around her like the sun.

She ran, impelled by racking pain,
    Through rugged ways and waters wild;
Where art thou, guardian spirit, fled?
    Oh haste to save an only child!

Hold!—he who doats on earthly things,
    'Tis fit their frailty should appear;
Hold!—they who providence accuse,
    'Tis just their folly cost them dear.

The God who guides the gilded moon,
    And rules the rough and rolling sea,
Without a trial ne'er will leave
    A soul to evil destiny.

When crossing Méggat's highland strand,
    She stopt to hear an eldritch scream;
Loud crew the cock at Henderland,
    The charm evanished like a dream!

The magic lanthorn left her head,
    And darkling now return she must.
She wept, and cursed her hapless doom;
    She wept, and called her God unjust.

But on that sad revolving day,
    The racking pains again return;
Ah, must we view a slave to lust,
    The bonny lass of Craigyburn?

Or see her to her father's hall,
    Returning, rueful, ruined quite:
And still, on that returning day,
    Yield to a monster's hellish might?

No—though harrassed, and sore distressed,
    Both shame and danger she endured;—
For heaven in pity interposed,
    And still her virtue was secured.

But o'er the scene we'll draw a veil,
    Wet with the tender tear of woe;
We'll turn, and view the dire effects
    From this nocturnal rout that flow:

For every month the spectre ran,
    With shrieks would any heart appal;
And every man and mother's son,
    Astonished fled at evening fall.

A bonny widow went at night
   To meet the lad she loved so well;
" Ah, yon's my former husband's sprite!"
   She said, and into faintings fell.

An honest taylor leaving work,
   Met with the lass of Craigyburn;
It was enough—he breathed his last!
   One shriek had done the taylor's turn.

But drunken John of Keppelgill
   Met with her on Carrifran gans;
He, staggering, cried, " Who devil's that?"
   Then plashing on, cried, "Faith, God kens!"

A mountain preacher quat his horse,
   And prayed aloud with lengthened phiz;
The damsel yelled—the father smelled—
   Dundee was but a joke to this.

Young Linton, in the Chapelhope,
   Enraged to see the road laid waste,
Way-laid the damsel with a gun,
   But in a panic home was chaced.

The Cameronians left their camp,
   And scattered wide o'er many a hill;
Pursued by men, pursued by hell,
   They stoutly held their tenets still.

But at the source of Moffat's stream,
   Two champions of the cov'nant dwell,
Who long had braved the power of men,
   And fairly beat the prince of hell:

Armed with a gun, a rowan-tree rung,
   A bible, and a scarlet twine,
They placed them on the Birkhill path,
   And distant saw the lanthorn shine.

And nearer, nearer, still it drew,
   At length they heard her piercing cries;
And louder, louder, still they prayed,
   With aching heart, and upcast eyes!

The bible, spread upon the brae,
   No sooner did the light illume,
Then straight the magic lanthorn fled,
   And left the lady in the gloom.

With open book, and haggart look,
"Say what art thou?" they loudly cry;
"I am a woman;—let me pass,
Or quickly at your feet I'll die.

"O let me run to Mary's kirk,
Where, if I'm forced to sin and shame,
A gracious God will pardon me;—
My heart was never yet to blame."

Armed with the gun, the rowan-tree rung,
The bible, and the scarlet twine,
With her they trudged to Mary's kirk,
This cruel sorcery out to find.

When nigh Saint Mary's isle they drew,
Rough winds and rapid rains began;
The livid lightning linked flew,
And round the rattling thunder ran:

The torrents rush, the mountains quake,
The sheeted ghosts run to and fro;
And deep, and long, from out the lake,
The Water-Cow was heard to low.

The mansion then seemed in a blaze,
   And issued forth a sulphurous smell;
An eldritch laugh went o'er their heads,
   Which ended in a hellish yell.

Bauld Halbert ventured to the cell,
   And, from a little window, viewed
The priest and Satan, close engaged
   In hellish rites, and orgies lewd.

A female form of melting wax,
   Mess John surveyed with steady eye,
Which ever and anon he pierced,
   And forced the lady loud to cry.

Then Halbert raised his trusty gun,
   Was loaded well with powder and ball;
And, aiming at the monster's head,
   He blew his brains against the wall.

The devil flew with such a clap,
   On door nor window did not stay;
And loud he cried, in jeering tone,
   " Ha, ha, ha, ha, poor John's away!"

East from the kirk and holy ground,
  They bare that lump of sinful clay,
And o'er him raised a mighty mound,
  Called Binram's Corse unto this day.

And ay when any lonely wight
  By yon dark cleugh is forced to stray,
He hears that cry at dead of night,
" Ha, ha, ha, ha, poor John's away."

NOTES

ON

MESS JOHN.

───

Mess John stood in Saint Mary's kirk.
                                         P. 71. v. 1.

The ruins of St Mary's chapel are still visible, in a wild scene on the banks of the lake of that name; but the mansion in which the priest, or, as some call him, the curate, lived, was almost erazed of late, for the purpose of building a stone-wall round the old church and burying-ground. This chapel is, in some ancient records, called *The Maiden Kirk*, and, in others, *The kirk of St Mary of the Lowes.*

His stature like the graceful pine,
  That grew on Bourhop-hills so high.
                                         P. 71. v. 3.

The hills of Bourhop, on the south side of the loch, opposite to the chapel, rise to the height of two thousand feet above the sea's level, and were, like much of that country, formerly covered with wood.

> *A silken mantle on her feet*
> *Fell down in many a fold and turn.*
>
> P. 74. v. 4.

It is a vulgar received opinion, that, let the devil assume what appearance he will, were it even that of an angel of light, yet still his feet must be cloven; and that, if he do not contrive some means to cover them, they will lead to a discovery of him and his intentions, which are only evil, and that continually. It is somewhat curious, that they should rank him amongst the clean beasts, which divide the hoof. They believe, likewise, that he and his emissaries can turn themselves into whatever shape they please, of all God's creatures, excepting those of a lion, a lamb, and a dove. Consequently their situation is the most perilous that can be conceived; for, when it begins to grow dark, they cannot be sure, but almost all the beasts and birds they see are either deils or witches. Of cats, hares, and swine, they are particularly jealous; and a caterwauling noise hath often turned men from going to see their sweethearts, and even from seeking the midwife. And I knew a girl, who returned home after proceeding ten miles on a journey, from the unlucky and ominous circumstance of an ugly bird crossing the road three times before her: Neither did her parents at all disapprove of what she had done.

> *You little know the fervid fires*
>   *In female breasts that burn so clear;*
> *The froward youth, of fierce desires,*
>   *To them is most supremely dear:*
> *Who ventures most to gain their charms,*
>   *By them is ever most approved;*
> *The ardent kiss, and clasping arms,*
>   *By them are ever best beloved.*—P. 75. v. 2. 3.

If any of my fair readers should quarrel with the sentiments manifested in these two stanzas, they will recollect that they are the sentiments of a fiend; who, we must suppose, was their mortal enemy, and would not scruple to paint their refined sensibility in very false colours, or, at least, from a very wrong point of view.

With fire and steel to urge her weel,
See that you neither stint nor spare.

P. 76. v. 1.

The story says, that the priest was obliged to watch the picture very constantly; and that always when the parts next the fire began to soften, he stuck pins into them, and exposed another side; that, when each of these pins were stuck in, the lady uttered a piercing shriek; and that, as their number increased in the waxen image, her torment increased, and caused her to haste on with amazing speed.

Where wild Polmoody's mountains tower,
Full many a wight their vigils keep.

P. 78. v. 2.

The mountains of Polmoody, besides being the highest, are the most inaccessible in the south of Scotland; and great numbers, from the western counties, found shelter on them during the heat of the persecution. Many of these, it is supposed, were obliged to shift for their sustenance by stealing sheep; yet the country people, from a sense that *Necessity has no law,* winked at the loss; their sheep being, in those days, of less value than their meal, of which they would otherwise have been obliged to part with a share to the sufferers. Part of an old ballad is still current in that neighbourhood, which relates their adventures, and the difficulties they laboured under for want of meat, and in getting hold of the sheep during the night. Some of the country people, indeed, ascribe these depredations to the persecutors; but it is not likely that they would put themselves to so much trouble. I remember only a few stanzas of this ballad, which are as follows:

* * * * *

 Caryfran Gan's they're very strait,
  We canna gang without a road;
 But tak' ye the tae side, an' me the tither,
  And they'll a' come in at Firthup Dod.

* * * * *

 On Turnberry and Caryfran Gan's,
  And out among the Moodlaw haggs,
 They worried the feck o' the laird's lambs,
  And eatit them raw, and buried the baggs.

* * * * *

 Had Guemsey's Castle a tongue to speak,
  Or mouth o' flesh, that it could fathom;
 It wad tell o' mony a supple trick,
  Was done at the foot o' Rotten-boddom:
 Where Donald, and his hungry men,
  Oft hough'd them up wi' little din;
 And, mair intent on flesh than yarn,
  Bure aff the bouk, and buried the skin.

This Guemseys is an extensive wild glen on the further side of these mountains; and being, in former times, used as a common, to which many of the gentlemen and farmers of Tweeddale drove their flocks to feed during the summer months, consequently it would be, at that season, a very fit place for a prey. The Donald mentioned may have been the famous Donald Cargill, a Cameronian preacher, of great notoriety at the period.

Where roars the torrent from Lochskene,
  A troop is lodged in trenches deep.—P. 78. v. 2.

There are sundry cataracts in Scotland, called *The Grey Mare's Tail;* in particular, one in the parish of Closeburn, in Nithsdale; and one betwixt Stranraer and Newton-Stewart: But that in Polmoody, on the border of Annandale, surpasses them all; as the water, with only one small intermission, falls from a height of 300 yards. This, with the rocks overhanging it on each side, when the water is flooded, greatly excels any thing I ever saw in awful grandeur. Immediately below it, in the straitest part of that narrow pass which leads from Annandale into Yarrow, a small strong entrenchment is visible. It is called by the country people, *The Giant's trench.* It is in the form of an octave, and is defended behind by a bank. As it is not nearly so much grown up as those at Philiphaugh, it is probable, that a handful of the covenanters might fortify themselves there during the time that their brethren were in arms. But it is even more probable, that a party of the king's troops might be posted for some time in that important pass; as it is certain, Claverhouse made two sweeping circuits of that country, and, the last time, took many prisoners in the immediate vicinity of this scene. May we not likewise suppose, that the outrage committed at Saint Mary's kirk might contribute to his appearance in those parts?

Young Linton in the Chapelhope,
  Enraged to see the road laid waste.—P. 81. v. 5.

The Lintons were, in those days, and even till toward the beginning of the last century, the principal farmers in all the upper parts of Ettrick and Yarrow; yet such a singular reverse of fortune have these opulent families experienced, that there is now rarely one of the name to be found above the rank of the meanest labourer. The Lintons of Chapel-hope either favoured or pitied the covenanters; for they fed and sheltered great numbers of them, even to the impairing of their fortunes. On Dundee's first approach to these parts, Mrs Linton went out to the road, and invited him and all his men to partake of a liberal refreshment, which they thankfully accepted; and this being a principal family, he went away so thoroughly convinced of the attachment of that neighbourhood to the royal cause, that a scrutiny was not only, at that time, effectually prevented, but the troops returned no more there for many years, until the license which they there enjoyed gathered such numbers as to become quite notorious. The spots where conventicles were held on these grounds, are still well known, and pointed out by some devout shepherds, with anecdotes of the preachers, or some of the principal characters. One can scarcely believe, but that Mr Graham had visited these spots, or was present on them, when he wrote the following lines:

"O'er hills, through woods, o'er dreary wastes, they sought
The upland moors, where rivers, there but brooks,
Dispart to different seas. Fast by such brooks,
A little glen is sometimes scooped; a plat
With green-sward gay, and flowers, that strangers seem
Amid the heathery wild, that all around
Fatigues the eye."——

These lines, with the two following pages of the sweet poem in which they occur, seem to be literal sketches of these scenes, as well as a representation of the transactions which then took place: For years more gloomy followed; and, from these "green-swards gay," they were driven into the "deep dells, by rocks o'er-canopied." Thus, it was high up in Ryskinhope where Renwick preached his last sermon, above the lakes, the sources of the Yarrow, where there is neither plat nor plain, but linns and moors. When he prayed that day few of the hearers' cheeks were dry. My parents were well acquainted with a woman whom he there baptized.

But at the source of Moffat's stream,
  Two champions of the cov'nant dwell;
Who long had braved the power of men,
  And fairly beat the prince of hell.—P. 82. v. 2.

These mens names were Halbert Dobson, and David Dun; better known by those of Hab Dob, and Davie Din. The remains of their cottage is still visible, and sure never was human habitation contrived on such a spot. It is on the very brink of a precipice, which is 400 feet perpendicular height, whilst another of half that height overhangs it above. To this they resorted, in times of danger, for a number of years; and the precipice is still called *Dob's linn*.

There is likewise a natural cavern in the bottom of the linn farther up, where they, with other ten, hid themselves for several days, while another kept watch upon the Pathknow; and they all assembled at the cottage during the night.

Tradition relates farther of these two champions, that, while they resided at the cottage by themselves, the devil appeared to them every night, and plagued them exceedingly; striving often to terrify them, so as to make them throw themselves over the linn. But one day they contrived a hank of red yarn in the form of crosses, which it was impossible the devil could pass; and, on his appearance at night, they got in behind him, and attacked him resolutely with each a bible in one hand, and a rowan-tree staff in the other, and, after a desperate encounter, they succeeded in tumbling him headlong over the linn; but, to prevent hurting himself, at the moment he was overcome, he turned himself into a batch of skins! It was not those of stolen sheep we hope. Credulity has been the ruling passion of the Scots at this time, else such a story never could have obtained the least credit; yet, it is said, these men were wont to tell it as long as they lived, concluding it always with the observation, that the devil had never more troubled them, as he found it was not for his health. A short rhyme is still extant relating to this singular tradition; but which seems to have been composed afterwards, as the linn is there called Dob's linn. It seems not improbable, that the bard who composed the song above quoted was likewise the author of this, for, like it, it is hard to say whether it is serious or burlesque.

> Little kend the wirrikow,
> What the covenant could dow!
> What o' faith, an' what o' fen,
> What o' might, an' what o' men;
> Or he had never shewn his face,
> His reekit rags, and riven taes,*
> To men o' mak, an' men o' mense,
> Men o' grace, an' men o' sense:
> For Hab Dob, and Davie Din,
> Dang the deil owre Dob's linn.
>
> Weir quo' he, an' weir quo' he;
> Haud the bible till his e'e;
> Ding him owre, or thrush him down,
> He's a fause deceitfu' lown!—
> Then he owre him, an' he owre him,
> He owre him, an' he owre him:
> Habby held him griff and grim,
> Davie threush him liff an' limb;

---

* The " reekit duds, and reistit phiz," which Burns attributes to the grand enemy of mankind, is perhaps borrowed from this popular rhyme.

> Till, like a bunch o' barkit skins,
> Down flew Satan ower the linns.

After seeing this, the reader will not deny, that our champions " fairly beat the prince of hell."

> *And deep and long, from out the lake,*
> *The Water-Cow was heard to low.*—P. 83. v. 5.

In some places of the Highlands of Scotland, the inhabitants are still in continual terror of an imaginary being, called *The Water-Horse.* When I was travelling over the extensive and dreary isle of Lewis, I had a lad of Stornoway with me as a guide and interpreter. On leaving the shores of Loch Rogg, in our way to Harries, we came to an inland lake, called, I think, Loch Alladale; and, though our nearest road lay alongst the shores of this loch, Malcolm absolutely refused to accompany me by that way for fear of the *Water-Horse,* of which he told many wonderful stories, swearing to the truth of them; and, in particular, how his father had lately been very nigh taken by him, and that he had succeeded in decoying one man to his destruction, a short time previous to that. This spectre is likewise an inhabitant of Loch Aven at the foot of Cairngorm, and of Loch Laggan, in the wilds betwixt Lochaber and Badenoch. Somewhat of a similar nature seems to have been *The Water-Cow,* which, in former times, haunted Saint Mary's loch, of which some extremely fabulous stories are yet related; and, though rather less terrible and malevolent than the Water-Horse, yet, like him, she possessed the rare slight of turning herself into whatever shape she pleased, and was likewise desirous of getting as many dragged into the lake as possible. Andrew Moore, above-mentioned, said, that, when he was a boy, his parents would not suffer him to go to play near the loch for fear of her; and that he remembered of seeing her once coming swimming towards him and his comrades in the evening twilight, but they all fled, and she sunk before reaching the side. A farmer of Bourhope once got a breed of her, which he kept for many years, until they multiplied exceedingly; and he never had any cattle throve so well, until once, on some outrage or disrespect on the farmer's part towards them, the old dam came out of the lake one pleasant March evening, and gave such a roar, until all the surrounding hills shook again; upon which her progeny, nineteen in number, followed her all quietly into the loch, and were never more seen.

Which forced the lady loud to cry.—P. 84. v. 3.

After the subject of a ballad is fairly introduced, great particularity is disgusting; therefore, the lass of Craigyburn, after this line, is no more mentioned: But the story adds, that she died of a broken heart, and of the heats which she got in being forced to run so fast. Another tradition, which I heard more lately, says, that she was conveyed secretly to a nunnery in Ireland, and that her father, whose name was Nicolson, afterwards lived in Craikbeck.

THE DEATH OF DOUGLAS, LORD OF LIDDISDALE.

THE first stanza of this Song, as well as the history of the event to which it refers, is preserved by Hume of Godscroft in his history of the House of Douglas. The author having been successful in rescuing some excellent old songs from the very brink of oblivion, searched incessantly many years after the remains of this, until lately, by mere accident, he lighted upon a few scraps, which he firmly believes to have formed a part of that very ancient ballad. The reader may judge for himself. The first verse is from Hume; and all those printed within brackets are as near the original as rhyme and reason will permit. They are barely sufficient to distinguish the strain in which the old song hath proceeded.

THE DEATH

OF

DOUGLAS, LORD OF LIDDISDALE.

The Lady Douglas left her bower,
 An' ay sae loud as she did call,
" 'Tis all for gude Lord Liddisdale
 That I do let these tears down fall."

[" O haud your tongue, my sister dear,
 An' o' your weepin' let me be:
Lord Liddisdale will haud his ain
 Wi' ony Lord o' Chrystendie.

F.

" For him ye widna weep or whine
  If you had seen what I did see,]
That day he broke the troops o' Tyne,
  Wi's gilded sword o' metal free.

" Stout Heezlebrae was wonder wae
  To see his faintin' vassals yield;
An' in a rage he did engage
  Lord Liddisdale upon the field.

' Avaunt, thou haughty Scot,' he cry'd,
  ' Nor dare to face a noble fae;
Say—wilt thou brave the deadly brand,
  And heavy hand of Heezlebrae?'

" The word was scarcely mixt wi' air,
  When Douglas' sword his answer gae;
An' frae a wound, baith deep and sair,
  Out fled the soul o' Heezlebrae.

" Mad Faucet next, wi' wounds transfixt,
  In anguish gnaw'd the bloody clay;
Then Hallinshed he wheil'd an' fled,
  An' left his rich, ill-gotten prey.

" I ha'e been west, I ha'e been east,
   I ha'e seen dangers many a ane;
But for a bauld and dauntless breast,
   Lord Liddisdale will yield to nane.

" An' were I call'd to face the foe,
   An' bidden chuse my leader free;
Lord Liddisdale would be the man
   Should lead me on to victory.

[" O haud your tongue, my brother John!
   Though I have heard you patientlie,
Lord Liddisdale is dead an' gone,
   An' he was slain for love o' me.

" My little true an' trusty page
   Has brought the heavy news to me,
That my ain lord did him engage
   Where he could nouther ficht nor flee.

" Four o' the foremost men he slew,
   An' four he wounded despratelie;
But cruel Douglas came behind,
   An' ran him through the fair bodie.]

" O wae be to the Ettrick wood !
  O wae be to the banks of Ale !
O wae be to the dastard croud
  That murder'd handsome Liddisdale !

[" It wasna rage for Ramsey slain
  That rais'd the deadly feid sae hie ;]
Nor perjur'd Murray's timeless death—
  It was for kindness shewn to me.

[" When I was led through Liddisdale,
  An' thirty horsemen guarding me ;
When that gude lord came to my aid,
  Sae soon as he did set me free !]

" The wild bird sang, and woodlands rang,
  An' sweet the sun shone on the vale ;
Then thinkna ye my heart was wae
  To part wi' gentle Liddisdale.

" But I will greet for Liddisdale,
  Until my twa black een rin dry ;
An' I will wail for Liddisdale,
  As lang as I ha'e voice to cry.

"An' for that gude lord I will sigh
    Until my heart an' spirit fail;
An', when I die, O bury me
    On the left side of Liddisdale."

"Now haud your tongue, my sister dear,
    Your grief will cause baith dule an' shame;
Since ye were fause, in sic a cause,
    The Douglas' rage I canna blame."

"Gae stem the bitter norlan' gale;
    Gae bid the wild wave cease to rowe;
I'll own my love for Liddisdale
    Afore the king, my lord, an' you."

He drew his sword o' stained steel,
    While neid-fire gleam'd frae ilka eye,
Nor pity, nor remorse did feel,
    Till dead she at his feet did lye.

"O cruel man! what ha'e I done?
    I never wrong'd my lord nor thee;
I little thought my brother John
    Could ha'e the heart to murder me."

Sunk was her een, her voice was gane,
    Her bonny face was pale as clay,
Her hands she rais'd to heaven for grace;
    Then fainted, sunk, and died away.

He dight his sword upon the ground;
    Wi' tentless glare his een did rowe,
Till fixing on the throbbing wound
    That stain'd her breast of purest snow.

He cry'd, " O lady, fause an' fair !
    Now thou art dead and I undone !
I'll never taste of comfort mair,
    Nor peace of mind, aneath the sun !

" Owr mountains, seas, an' burnin' sand,
    I'll seek the plains of Italie;
Then kneel in Judah's distant land,
    An' syne come back an' sleep wi' thee."

WILLIE WILKIN.

The real name of this famous warlock was Johnston; how he came to acquire that of Wilkin I can get no information, though his name and his pranks are well known in Annandale and Nithsdale. He seems to have been an abridgement of Mr Michael Scott; but, though his powers were exhibited on a much more narrow scale, they were productive of actions yet more malevolent.

The glow-worm goggled on the moss
   When Wilkin rode away,
And much his aged mother fear'd,
   But wist not what to say.

For near the change of every moon,
   At deepest midnight tide,
He hied him to yon ancient fane
   That stands by Kinnel side.

His thoughts were absent, wild his looks,
   His speeches fierce and few;
But who he met, or what was done,
   No mortal ever knew.

" O stay at home, my only son!
   O stay at home with me!
I fear I'm secretly forewarn'd
   Of ills awaiting thee.

" Last night I heard the dead-bell sound,
   When all were fast asleep;
And ay it rung, and ay it sung,
   Till all my flesh did creep.

" And when on slumber's silken couch,
   My senses dormant lay,
I saw a pack of hungry hounds,
   Would make of thee their prey.

" With feeble step I ran to help,
 Or death with thee to share;
When straight you bound my hands and feet,
 And left me lying there.

" I saw them tear thy vitals forth;
 Thy life-blood dyed the way;
I saw thy eyes all glaring red,
 And closed mine for ay.

" Then stay at home, my only son!
 O stay at home with me!
Or take with thee this little book,
 Thy guardian it shall be."

" Hence, old fanatic, from my sight!
 What means this senseless whine?
I pray thee mind thine own affairs,
 Let me attend to mine."

" Alas, my son! the generous spark
 That warm'd thy tender mind
Is now extinct, and malice keen
 Is only left behind.

" How canst thou rend that aged heart
   That yearns thy woes to share?
Thou still hast been my only grief,
   My only hope and care.

" Ere I had been one month a bride,
   Of joy I took farewell;
With Craigie, on the banks of Sark,
   Thy valiant father fell.

" I nurs'd thee on my tender breast,
   With meikle care and pain;
And saw, with pride, thy mind expand,
   Without one sordid stain.

" With joy, each night, I saw thee kneel
   Before the throne of grace;
And on thy Saviour's blessed day
   Frequent his holy place.

" But all is gone! the vespers sweet
   Which from our castle rose
Are silent now, and sullen pride
   In hand with envy goes!

" Thy wedded wife has sway'd thy heart
    To pride and passion fell;
O! for thy pretty children's sake,
    Renounce that path of hell.

" Then stay at home, my only son!
    O with thy mother stay!
Or tell me what thou goest about,
    That for thee I may pray."

He turn'd about, and hasted out,
    And for his horse did call;
" An hundred fiends my patience rend,
    But thou excell'st them all."

She slipt beneath his saddle lap
    A book of psalms and pray'rs,
And hasten'd to yon ancient fane,
    To listen what was there.

And when she came to yon kirk-yard,
    Where graves are green and low,
She saw full thirty coal-black steeds
    All standing in a row.

Her Willie's was the tallest steed,
　'Twixt Dee and Annan whole;
But plac'd beside that mighty rank,
　He kyth'd but like a foal.

She laid her hand upon his side;
　Her heart grew cold as stone!
The cold sweat ran from every hair,
　He trembled every bone!

She laid her hand upon the next,
　His bulky side to stroak,
And ay she reach'd, and ay she stretch'd,—
　Was nothing all but smoke.

It was a mere delusive form
　Of films and sulphry wind;
And every wave she gave her hand
　A gap was left behind.

She pass'd through all those stately steeds,
　Yet nothing marr'd her way,
And left her shape in every shade,
　For all their proud array.

But whiles she felt a glowing heat,
    Though mutt'ring holy prayer;
And filmy veils assail'd her face,
    And stifling brimstone air.

Then for her darling desperate grown,
    Straight to the aisle she flew;
But what she saw, and what she heard,
    No mortal ever knew.

But yells, and moans, and heavy groans,
    And blackest blasphemye,
Did fast abound; for every hound
    Of hell seem'd there to be.

And after many a horrid rite,
    And sacrifice prophane,
" A book! a book!" they loudly howl'd;
    " Our spells are all in vain.

" Hu! tear him, tear him limb from limb,"
    Resounded through the pile,
" Hu! tear him, tear him straight, for he
    Has mock'd us all this while."

The tender matron, desperate grown,
　　Then shriek'd most bitterlye:
" O spare my son, and take my life,
　　The book was lodg'd by me."

" Ha! that's my frantic mother's voice!
　　My life or peace must end;
O take her! take her!" loud he cried,
　　" Take her, and spare thy friend!"

The riot rout then sallied out,
　　Like hounds upon their prey;
And gathered round her in the aisle,
　　With many a hellish bray.

Each angry shade endeavours made
　　Their fangs in blood to stain,
But all their efforts to be felt
　　Were impotent and vain.

Whether the wretched mortal there
　　His filial hands embrued,
Or if the ruler of the sky
　　The scene with pity view'd,—

And sent the streaming bolt of heaven,
　　Ordained to interpose,
To take her life, and save her soul,
　　From these infernal foes.

No man can tell, how it befel;
　　Enquiry all was vain;
But thence she never more returned,
　　She there that night was slain.

And Willie Wilkin's noble steed
　　Lay stiff upon the green.
A night so dire in Annandale
　　Before had never been!

Loud thunders shook the vault of heaven,
　　The bolts with fury flew;
The graves were plow'd, the rocks were riven;
　　Whole flocks and herds it slew.

They gather'd up her mangled limbs,
　　And laid beneath a stone;
But heart, and tongue, and every palm
　　From every hand were gone.

Her brains were dash'd against the wall,
    Her blood upon the floor;
Her reverend head, with sorrows grey,
    Hung on the chapel door.

To Auchineastle Wilkin hied,
    On Evan braes so green;
And liv'd and died like other men,
    For aught that could be seen.

But gloomy, gloomy was his look;
    And froward was his way;
And malice every action rul'd
    Until his dying day.

And many a mermaid staid his call,
    And many a mettled fay;
And many a wayward spirit learn'd
    His summons to obey.

And many a wondrous work he wrought,
    And many things foretold;
Much was he fear'd, but little lov'd,
    By either young or old.

NOTES

ON

WILLIE WILKIN.

He hied him to yon ancient fane
  That stands by Kinnel side.—P. 104. v. 1.

The name of this ancient fane is Dumgree. It is beautifully situated on the west side of the Kinnel, one of the rivers which joins the Annan from the west, and is now in ruins. It is still frequented by a few peaceable spirits at certain seasons. As an instance: Not many years ago, a neighbouring farmer, riding home at night upon a mare, who, besides knowing the road well enough, had her foal closed in at home, thought himself hard at his own house, but was surprised to find that his mare was stopped at the door of the old kirk of Dumgree. He mounted again, and essayed it a second and a third time; but always, when he thought himself at home, he found himself at the door of the old church of Dumgree, and farther from home than when he first set out. He was now sensible, that the beast was led by some invisible hand, so alighting, he went into the chapel and said his prayers; after which, he mounted, and rode as straight home as if it had been noon. If the farmer had told his story to my uncle Toby, he would certainly have whistled *Lillabullero*.

> *To Auchencastle Wilkin hied,*
>   *On Evan braes so green.*—P. 112. v. 2.

Auchencastle is situated on the west side of the Evan, another of the tributary streams of the Annan. It seems to have been a place of great strength and antiquity; is surrounded by a moat and a fosse, and is, perhaps, surpassed by none in Scotland for magnitude.

> *And lived and died like other men,*
>   *For aught that could be seen*—P. 112. v. 2.

If he lived and died like other men, it appears that he was not at all buried like other men. When on his death-bed, he charged his sons, as they valued their peace and prosperity, to sing no requiem, nor say any burial-service over his body; but to put a strong withie to each end of his coffin, by which they were to carry him away to Dumgree, and see that all the attendants were well mounted. On the top of a certain eminence they were to set down the corpse and rest a few minutes, and if nothing interfered they might proceed. If they fulfilled these, he promised them the greatest happiness and prosperity for four generations; but, if they neglected them in one point, the utmost misery and wretchedness. The lads performed every thing according to their father's directions; and they had scarcely well set down the corpse on the place he mentioned, when they were alarmed by the most horrible bellowing of bulls; and instantly two dreadful brindered ones appeared, roaring, and snuffing, and tossing up the earth with their horns and hoofs; on which the whole company turned and fled. When the bulls reached the coffin, they put each of them one of their horns into their respective withies, and ran off with the corpse, stretching their course straight to the westward. The relatives, and such as were well mounted, pursued them, and kept nigh them for several miles; but when they came to the small water of Brann, in Nithsdale, the bulls went straight through the air from the one hill head to the other, without descending to the bottom of the glen. This unexpected manœuvre threw the pursuers quite behind, though they need not have expected any thing else, having before observed, that their feet left no traces on the ground, though ever so soft. However, by dint of whip and spur, they again got sight of them; but when they came to Loch Ettrick, on the heights of Closeburn, they had all lost sight of them but two, who were far behind: but the bulls there meeting with another company, plunged into the lake with the corpse, and were never more seen at that time. Ever since, his spirit has haunted that loch, and continues to do so to this day.

He was, when alive, very fond of the game of curling on the ice, at which no mortal man could beat him; nor has his passion for it ceased with death; for he and his hellish confederates continue to amuse themselves with this game during the long winter nights, to the great terror and annoyance of the neighbourhood, not much regarding whether the loch be frozen or not. I have heard sundry of the neighbouring inhabitants declare, with the most serious countenances, that they have heard them talking, and the sound of the stones running alongst the ice and hitting each other, as distinctly as ever they did when present at a real and substantial curling. Some have heard him laughing, others lamenting; and others have seen the two bulls plashing and swimming about in the loch at the close of the evening. In short, every one allows it to be a dangerous place, and a place where very many have been affrighted; though there is little doubt that, by making allowances for the magnifying qualities of fear, all the above might be accounted for in a natural way.—Wilkin's descendants are still known; and the poorer sort of them have often their great predecessor mentioned to them as a term of reproach, whom they themselves allow to have been an *awesome body*.

THIRLESTANE.

A FRAGMENT.

Sir Robert Scott, knight of Thirlestane, was first married to a lady of high birth and qualifications, whom he most tenderly loved; but she, soon dying, left him an only son. He was afterwards married to a lady of a different temper, by whom he had several children; whose jealousy of the heir made Sir Robert doat still more on this darling son. She, knowing that the right of inheritance belonged to him, and that, of course, a very small share would fall to her sons, seeing he loved the heir so tenderly, grew every year more uneasy. But the building, and other preparations which were going on at Gamescleuch, on the other side of the Ettrick, for his accommodation on reaching his majority, when he was also to be married to a fair kinswoman, drove her past all patience, and made her resolve on his destruction. The masonry of his new castle of Gamescleuch was finished on his birth-day, when he reached his twentieth year, but it never went farther. This being always a feast-day at Thirlestane, the lady prepared, on that day, to put her hellish plot in execution; for which purpose, she had previously secured to her interest John Lally, the family piper. This man, tradition says, procured her three adders, of which they chose the parts replete with most deadly poison; these they ground to a fine powder, and mixed with a bottle of wine. On the forenoon before the festival commenced, he went over to Gamescleuch to regale his workmen, who had exerted themselves to get their work finished on that day, and Lally the piper went with him as server. When his young lord called for wine to drink a health to the masons, John gave him a cup of the poisoned bottle, which he drank off. Lally went out of the castle, as if about to return home; but that was the last sight of him. He could never be found, nor heard of, though the most diligent and extended search was made for him. The heir swelled and burst almost instantaneously. A large company of the then potent name of Scott, with others, were now assembled at Thirlestane to grace the festival; but what a woeful meeting it turned out to be! They with one voice pronounced him poisoned; but where to attach the blame remained a mystery, as he was so universally loved and esteemed. The first thing the knight caused to be done, was blowing the blast on the trumpet or great bugle, which was the warning for all the family instantly to assemble, which they did in the court of the castle. He then put the following question: " Now, are we all here?" A voice answered from the crowd, " We are all here but Lally the piper." Simple and natural as this answer may seem, it served as an electrical shock to old Sir Robert. It is supposed that, knowing the confidence which his lady placed in this menial, the whole scene of cruelty opened to his eyes at once; and the trying conviction, that his peace was destroyed by her most dear to him, struck so forcibly upon his feelings, that it totally deprived him of reason. He stood a long time speechless, and then fell to repeating the answer which he received, like one half awakened out of a sleep; nor was he ever heard, for many a day, to speak another word than these, " We're all here but Lally the piper:" And when any one accosted him, whatever was the subject, that was sure to be the answer he received.

The method which he took to revenge his son's death was singular and unwarrantable: He said, that the estate of right belonged to his son, and since he could not bestow it upon him living, he would spend it all upon him now he was dead; and that neither the lady nor her children should ever enjoy a farthing of that which she had played so foully for. The body was accordingly embalmed, and lay in great splendour at Thirlestane for a year and a day; during all which time Sir Robert kept open house, welcoming and feasting all who chose to come, and actually spent or mortgaged his whole estate, saving a very small patrimony in Eskdale-muir, which belonged to his wife. Some say, that while all the country who chose to come were thus feasting at Thirlestane, she remained shut up in a vault of the castle, and lived on bread and water.

During the three last days of this wonderful feast, the crowds which gathered were immense; it seemed as if the whole country were assembled at Thirlestane. The butts of wine were carried to the open fields, the ends knocked out of them with hatchets, stones, or whatever came readiest to hand, and the liquor carried about " in stoups and in caups." On these days the burn of Thirlestane ran constantly red with wine, and even communicated its tincture to the river Ettrick. The family vault, where his corpse was interred in a leaden chest, is under the same roof with the present parish church of Ettrick, and distant from Thirlestane about a Scots mile. To give some idea of the magnitude of the burial, the old people tell us, that though the whole way was crowded with attendants, yet, when the leaders of the procession reached the church, the rearmost were not nearly got from Thirlestane.

Sir Robert, shortly after dying, left his family in a state little short of downright beggary, which, they say, the lady herself came to before she died. As Sir Robert's first lady was of the family of Harden, some suspected him of having a share in forwarding the knight's desperate procedure. Certain it is, however, he did not, in this instance, depart from the old family maxim, "*Keep what you have, and catch what you can,*" but made a noble hand of the mania of grief which so overpowered the faculties of the old baron; for when accounts came to be cleared up, a large proportion of the lands turned out to be Harden's. And it is added, on what authority I know not, that when the extravagance of Sir William Scott obliged the Harden family to part with these lands, the purchasers were bound, by the bargain, to refund these lands, should the Scotts of Thirlestane ever make good their right to them, either by law or redemption.

The nearest lineal descendant from this second marriage is one Robert Scott, a poor man who lives at the Binks on Teviot, whom the generous Buccleuch has taken notice of and provided for. He is commonly distinguished by the appellation of *Rob the Laird,* from the conviction of what he would have been had he got fair play. With this man, who is very intelligent, I could never find an opportunity of conversing, though I sought it diligently. It is said, he can inform as to many particulars relating to this sad catastrophe; and that, whenever he has occasion to mention a certain great predecessor of his, (the lady of Thirlestane) he distinguishes her by the uncouth epithet of the d——d b——h. It must be remarked, that I had access to no records for the purpose of ascertaining the facts above stated, though I believe they are for the most part pretty correct. Perhaps much might be learned by applying to the noble representative of the family, the Honourable Lord Napier, who is still possessed of the beautiful mountains round Thirlestane, and who has it at present in contemplation to rebuild and beautify it; which may God grant him health and prosperity to accomplish.—It is to this story that the following fragment relates.

THIRLESTANE.

A FRAGMENT.

Fer, fer hee raide, and fer hee gaed,
   And aft he sailit the sea;
And thrise he crossit the Alpyne hills
   To distant Italie.

Beyon Lough-Ness his tempil stude,
   Ane ril of meikle fame;
A knight of gude Seant John's hee was,
   And Baldwin was his name.

By wonderous lore hee did explore
   What after tymes wald bee;
And manie mystic links of fate
   He hafflins culd fursee.

Fer, fer hee raide, and fer hee gaed,
    Owr mony hill and dale;
Till, passing through the fair foreste,
    He learnit a waesom tale.

Wher Ettrick wandirs down a plain,
    With lofty hills belay't,
The staitly towirs of Thirlestane
    With wundir hee surveyt.

Black hung the bannir on the wall;
    The trumpit seimit to grane;
And reid, reid ran the bonny burn,
    Whilk erst like siller shone.

At first a noise like fairie soundis
    He indistinctly heard;
Then countless, countless were the crouds
    Whilke round the walls appeir'd.

Thousands of steids stood on the hill,
    Of sable trappings vaine;
And round on Ettricks baittle haughs
    Grew no kin kind of graine.

Hee gazit, he wonderit, sair he fearit
   Sum recent tragedie;
At lenth he spyit ane woeful wight
   Gaun droopin on the ley.

His beard was silverit owr wi' eild;
   Pale was his cheek wae-worn;
His hayre was like the muirland wild
   On a December morn.

" Haile, revirent brither," Baldwin said,
   " Here, in this unco land,
A temple warrior greets thee well,
   And offers thee his hand.

" O tell me why the peepill murn?
   Sure all is not for gude:
And why, why does the bonnie burn
   Rin reid wi' Christian blude?"

Ald Beattie turnit and shuke his heid,
   While down fell mony a teir;
" O wellcom, wellcom, sire," he said,
   " Ane waesum tale to heire:

" The gude Sir Robert's sonne and aire
  By creuel handis lyis slain;
And all his wide domains, so fair,
  To ither lords ar gane.

" On sik ane youth as him they mourn,
  The sun did never shine;—
Instead of Christian blude, the burn
  Rins reid wi' Renis wine.

" This is the sad returnin day
  He first beheld the light;
This is the sad returnin day
  He fell by cruel spite.

" And on this day, with pomp and pride,
  From hence you'll see him borne;
And his poor faither sad return
  Of landis and onuris shorne.

" Come to my littill chambir still,
  In yonder turret low;
We'll say our praiers for the dead,
  And for the leeving too.

" And when thou hast a free repast
    Of wheat bread and the wine,
My tale shall weet thy onest cheeks,
    As oft it has dune mine."

* * * * * * *

LORD DERWENT.

A FRAGMENT.

" O why look ye so pale, my lord?
    And why look ye so wan?
  And why stand mounted at your gate,
    So early in the dawn?"

" O well may I look pale, lady;
    For how can I look gay,
  When I have fought the live-long night,
    And fled at break of day."

" And is the border troop arrived?
    And have they won the day?
  It must have been a bloody field,
    Ere Derwent fled away.

" But where got ye that stately steed,
 So stable and so good?
And where got ye that gilded sword,
 So dyed with purple blood?"

" I got that sword, in bloody fray,
 Last night on Eden downe;
I got the horse, and harnass too,
 Where mortal ne'er got one."

" Alight, alight, my noble lord;
 God mot you save and see!
For never, till this hour, was I
 Afraid to look on thee."

He turned him to the glowing east,
 That stained both tower and tree:
" Prepare, prepare, my lady fair,
 Prepare to follow me.

" Before this dawning day shall close,
 A deed shall here be done,
That men unborn shall shrink to hear,
 And dames the tale shall shun.

" The conscious morning blushes deep,
 The foul intent to see.
Prepare, prepare, my lady fair,
 Prepare to follow me."

" Alight, alight, my noble lord,
 I'll live or die with thee;
I see a wound deep in your side,
 And hence you cannot flee."

She looked out o'er her left shoulder
 To list a heavy groan;
But when she turned her round again,
 Her noble lord was gone.

She looked to east, and west, and south,
 And all around the tower;
Through house and hall, but man nor horse
 She never could see more.

She turned her round, and round about,
 All in a doleful state;
And there she saw her little foot page
 Alighting at the gate.

" Oh! open, open, noble dame,
    And let your servant in;
Our furious foes are hard at hand,
    The castle fair to win."

" But tell me, Billy, where's my lord?
    Or whither is he bound?
He's gone just now, and in his side
    A deep and deadly wound."

" Why do you rave, my noble dame,
    And look so wild on me?
Your lord lies on the bloody field,
    And him you'll never see.

" With Scottish Jardine, hand to hand,
    He fought most valiantly,
Put him to flight, and broke his men,
    With shouts of victory.

" But Maxwell rallying, wheeled about,
    And charged as fierce as hell;
Yet ne'er could pierce the English troop
    Till my brave master fell.

" Then all was gone; the ruffian Scot
 Bore down our flying band;
And now they waste, with fire and sword,
 The Links of Cumberland.

" Lord Maxwell's gone to Carlisle town,
 With Jardine bold and true;
And young Kilpatrick and Glencairn
 Are come in search of you."

" How dare you lie, my little page,
 Whom I pay meat and fee?
The cock has never crowed but once
 Since Derwent was with me.

" The bird that sits on yonder bush,
 And sings so loud and clear,
Has only three times changed his note
 Since my good lord was here."

" Whoe'er it was, whate'er it was,
 I'm sure it was not he:
I saw him slain on Eden plain,
 And him you'll never see.

" I saw him stand against an host,
    While heaps before him fell;
I saw them pierce his manly side,
    And bring his last farewell.

" O run! he cried, to my ladye,
    And bear the fray before;
Tell her I died for England's right—
    Then word spake never more.

" Come, let us fly to Westmoreland,
    For here you cannot stay;
We'll fairly shift; our steeds are swift;
    And well I know the way."

" I will not fly, I cannot fly;
    My heart is wonder sore;
My brain it turns, my blood it burns,
    And all with me is o'er."

She turned her eyes to Borrowdale;
    Her heart grew chill with dread,—
For there she saw the Scottish band,
    Kilpatrick at their head.

Red blazed the beacon on Pownell;
  On Skiddaw there were three;
The warder's horn, on muir and fell,
  Was heard continually.

Dark grew the sky, the wind was still,
  The sun in blood arose;
But oh! how many a gallant man
  Ne'er saw that evening close!

* * * * * * *

NOTES

ON

LORD DERWENT.

―――

I got that sword in bloody fray,
  Last night on Eden downe.—P. 129. v. 2.

This ballad relates to an engagement which took place betwixt the Scots and English, in Cumberland, A. D. 1524; for a particular account of which, see the historians of that time.

But Maxwell rallying, wheeled about.—P. 131. v. 5.

The page's account of this action seems not to be wide of the truth: " On the 17th of Julie, the Lord Maxwell, and Sir Alexander Jardein, with diverse other Scottishmen, in great numbers entered England by the west marches and Caerleill, with displayed banners, and began to harrie the country, and burn diverse places. The Englishmen assembled on every side, so that they were far more in number than the Scottishmen, and thereupon set feircielie upon their enemies: insomuch, that, for the space of an hour, there was a sore fight continued betwixt them. But the

Lord Maxwell, like a true politike captain, as of all that knew him he was no less reputed, ceased not to incourage his people; and after that, by the taking of Sir Alexander Jardein and others, they had beene put backe, he brought them in arraie again, and, beginning a new skirmish, recovered in manner all the prisoners; took and slew diverse Englishmen; so that he returned with victorie, and led above 300 prisoners with him into Scotland."—HOLINGSHED.

THE
LAIRD OF LAIRISTAN,
OR, THE
THREE CHAMPIONS OF LIDDISDALE.

The scene of this ballad is laid in the upper parts of Liddisdale, in ~~which district the~~ several residencies of the three champions are situated, as is also the old castle of Hermitage, with the farm-houses of Saughentree and Roughley.

As to the authenticity of the story, all that I can say of it is, that I used to hear it told when I was a boy, by William Scott, a joiner of that country, and was much taken with some of the circumstances. Were I to relate it verbatim, it would only be anticipating a great share of the poem.—One verse is ancient, beginning, O wae be to thee, &c.

THE LAIRD OF LAIRISTAN;

OR, THE

THREE CHAMPIONS OF LIDDISDALE.

"O WILLIE, 'tis light, and the moon shines bright,
 Will ye go and watch the deer wi' me?"
"Ay, be my sooth, this very night:"—
 And away they went to the Saughentree.

 The moon had turn'd the roof of heaven;
  The ground lay deep in drifted snaw;
 The hermitage bell had rung eleven,
  When lo! a wondrous sight they saw.

Right owr the knowe where Liddel lyes,—
    Nae wonder that it catch'd his ee!
A thing of huge and monstrous size
    Was steering that way hastilye.

" Ah! what is yon, my brother John?
    Now God preserve baith you and me!
But our guns they are load, and what comes in
        their road,
    Be't boggle, or robber, these bullets shall prie."

" Oh haud your tongue, my brother dear;
    Let us survey't with steedy ee;
'Tis surely a man they are carrying here,
    And 'tis fit that the family warn'd should be."

They ran to the ha', and they waken'd them a',
    Where none were at home but maidens three;
And into the shade of the wall they have staid,
    To watch what the issue of this would be.

And there they saw a dismal sight!
    A sight had neerly freez'd their blood!
One lost her reason that very night,
    And one of them fainted where they stood.

Four stalwart men, on arms so bright,
    Came bearing a corpse with many a wound;
His habit bespoke him a lord or knight;
    And his fair ringlets swept the ground.

They heard a voice to the other say—
    " A place to leave him will not be found;
The barn is lock'd, and the key away."—
    Said one, " In the byre we'll lay him down."

Then into the byre the corpse they bore,
    And away they fled right speedilye;
The rest took shelter within the door,
    In wild amazement, as well might be:

And into the byre no ane durst gang,
    No, not for the life of his bodye;
But the blood on the snaw was trail'd alang,
    And they kend a' wasna as it should be.

Next morning all the Dalesmen ran;
    For soon the word was far and wide;
And there lay the Laird of Lairistan,
    The bravest knight on the border side!

He was wounded behind, and wounded before,
  And cloven through the left cheek-bone;
And clad in the habit he daily wore;
  But his sword, and his belt, and his bonnet were gone.

Then east and west the word has gane,
  And soon to Branxholm ha' it flew,
That Elliot of Lairistan he was slain,
  And how or why no creature knew.

Buccleuch has mounted his milk-white steed,
  With fifteen knights in his companye;
To Hermitage Castle they rode with speed,
  Where all the dale was summon'd to be.

And soon they came, a numerous host,
  And they swore, and touch'd the dead bodie;
But Jocky o' Millburn he was lost,
  And could not be found in the hale countrye.

" Now, wae be to thee, Armstrong o' Millburn!
  And O an ill death may'st thou dee!
Through thee we have lost brave Lairistan,
  But his equal thou wilt never be.

"The Bewcastle men may ramp and rave,
 And drive away the Liddisdale kye:
For now is our guardian laid in his grave;
 And Branxholm and Thirlestane distant lye."

The Dales-men thus his loss deplore,
 And every one his virtues tell;
His hounds lay howling at the door;
 His hawks flew idle o'er the fell.

When three long years were come and gone,
 Two shepherds sat on Roughly hill;
And ay they sigh'd, and made their moan,
 O'er present times that look'd so ill.

" Our young king lives at London town,
 Buccleuch must bear him companye;
And Thirlestane's all to ruin gone,
 And who shall our protector be?

" And jealous of the Stuart race,
    The English lords begin to thraw;
The land is in a piteous case,
    When subjects rise against the law.

" Ere all is done, our blood may soak
    Our Scottish houms, and leave a stain—
A stain like that on Sundup's cloak,
    Which never will wash out again."

Amazement kyth'd in Sandy's face;
    His mouth to open wide began;
He star'd, and look'd from place to place,
    As events o'er his mem'ry ran.

The broider'd cloak of gaudy green
    That Sundup wore, and was sae gay,
For three lang years had ne'er been seen,
    At chapel, raid, nor holiday.

He minded too, he once o'erheard,
    (When courting of his bonny Ann)
A hint, the which he greatly fear'd,
    But ne'er could thoroughly understand.

" Now tell me, Willie, tell me true;
    Your sim'lie bodes us little good;
I fear the cloak you mention'd now—
    I fear 'tis stain'd with noble blood!"

" Indeed, my friend, you've guess'd aright;
    I never meant to tell to man
That tale; but crimes will come to light,
    Let human wits do what they can.

" But He, who ruleth wise and well,
    Hath order'd from his seat on high,
That ay since valiant Elliot fell
    That mantle bears the purple dye.

" And all the waters in Liddisdale,
    And all that lash the British shore,
Can ne'er wash out the wondrous maele!
    It still seems fresh with purple gore."

Then east and west the word has gane,
    And soon to Branxholm hall it flew;
And Halbert o' Sundup hee was ta'en,
    And brought before the high Buccleuch.

The cloak was hung in open hall,
    Where ladies and lords of high degree,
And many a one, both great and small,
    Were struck with awe the same to see.

" Now tell me, Sundup," said Buccleuch,
    " If this is rul'd by God on high?
If that is Elliot's blood we view,
    False Sundup! thou shalt surely die."

Then Halbert turn'd him where he stood,
    And wip'd the round tear from his ee;
" That blood, my lord, is Elliot's blood;
    I winna keep the truth frae thee."

" O ever-alack!" said good Buccleuch,
    " If that be true thou tell'st to me,
On the highest tree in Branxholm heuch,
    Stout Sundup, thou must hangit be."

" 'Tis Elliot's blood; I tell you true:
    And Elliot's death was wrought by me;
And were the deed again to do,
    I'd do't in spite of hell and thee.

" My sister, brave Jock Armstrong's bride,
 The fairest flower of Liddisdale,
By Elliot basely was betray'd;
 And roundly has he paid the mail.

" We watch'd him in her secret bower,
 And found her to his bosom prest;
He begg'd to have his broad claymore,
 And dar'd us both to do our best.

" Perhaps, my lord, ye'll truly say,
 In rage, from laws of arms we swerv'd:
Though Lairistan got double play,
 'Twas fairer play than he deserv'd.

" We might have kill'd him in the dark,
 When in the lady's arms lay he;
We might have kill'd him in his sark,
 Yet gave him room to fight or flee.

" Come on, then, gallant Milburn cry'd,
 My single arm shall do the deed;
Or heavenly justice is denied,
 Or that false heart of thine shall bleed.

" Then to't they fell, both sharp and snell,
    With steady hand and watchful eye;
Soon blood and sweat from either fell;
    And from their swords the sparkles fly.

" The first stroke Milburn to him wan,
    He ript his bosom to the bone;
Though Armstrong was a gallant man,
    Like Elliot living there was none.

" His growth was like the Border oak;
    His strength the bison's strength outvied;
His courage like the mountain rock;
    For skill his man he never tried.

" Oft had we three, in Border fray,
    Made chiefs and armies stand in awe;
And little thought to see the day,
    On other deadly thus to draw.

" The first wound that brave Milburn got,
    The tear of rage row'd in his ee;
The next stroke that brave Milburn got,
    The blood ran dreeping to his knee.

" My sword I grip'd into my hand,
 And fast to his assistance ran;—
What could I do? I could not stand
 And see the base deceiver win.

" O turn thee, turn thee, limmer loun!
 O turn and change a blow with me,
Or, by the righteous powers aboon,
 I'll hew the arm from thy bodye.

" He turn'd, with many a haughty word,
 And lounged and struck most furiouslye;
But with one slap of my broad sword
 I brought the traitor to his knee.

" Now take thou that, stout Armstrong cry'd,
 For all the pain thou'st gi'en to me;
(Though then he shortly would have died)
 And ran him through the fair bodye."

Buccleuch's stern look began to change;
   To tine a warrior lothe was he;
The crime was call'd a brave revenge,
   And Halbert of Sundup was set free.

Then every man for Milburn mourn'd,
   And wish'd him to enjoy his own;
But Milburn never more return'd
   Till ten long years were come and gone.

Then loud alarms through England ring,
   And deeds of death and dool began;
The commons rose against the king,
   And friends to diff'rent parties ran.

The nobles join the royal train,
   And soon his ranks with grandeur fill;
They sought their foes with might and main,
   And found them lying on Edgehill.

The trumpets blew, the bullets flew,
   And long and bloody was the fray;
At length o'erpower'd, the rebel crew
   Before the royal troops gave way.

" Who was the man," Lord Lindsey cry'd,
 " That fought so well through all the fray?
Whose coat of rags, together ty'd,
 Seems to have seen a better day?

" Such bravery in so poor array,
 I never in my life did see;
His valour three times turn'd the day,
 When we were on the point to flee."

Then up there spoke a man of note,
 Who stood beside his majestie,
" My liege, the man's a border Scot,
 Who volunteer'd to fight for thee."

The king he smil'd, and said aloud,
 " Go bring the valiant Scot to me;
When we have all our foes subdued,
 The Lord of Liddel he shall be."

The king gave him his gay gold ring,
 And made him there a belted knight;
But Milburn bled to save his king!
 The king to save his royal right!

SONGS

ADAPTED TO THE TIMES.

SANDY TOD.

A Scottish Pastoral.

TO A LADY.

―――

You ha'e learned in love to languish,
　You ha'e felt affliction's rod,
Murn wi' me the meltin' anguish,
　Murn the loss o' Sandy Tod.

Sandy was a lad o' vigour,
　Clean an' tight o' lith an' lim',
For a decent, manly figure,
　Few cou'd ding or equal him.

In a cottage, poor and nameless,
   By a little bouzy linn,
Sandy led a life sae blameless,
   Far frae ony strife or din.

Annan's fertile dale beyon' him,
   Spread her fields an' meadows green;
Hoary Hertfell towered aboon him,
   Smilin' to the sun—gude e'en.

Few his wants, his wishes fewer,
   Save his flocks nae care had he;
Never heart than his was truer,
   Tender to the last degree.

He was learned, and every tittle
   E'er he read believed it true;
Savin' chapters cross an' kittle,
   He cou'd read his bible through.

Oft he read the acts o' Joseph,
   How wi' a' his friends he met;
Ay the hair his noddle rose off,
   Ay his cheeks wi' tears were wet.

Seven bonny buskit simmers
   O'er the Solway Frith had fled,
Since a flock o' ewes an' gimmers
   Out amang the hills he fed.

Some might bragg o' knowledge deeper,
   But nae herd was lo'ed sae weel;
Sandy's hirsel proved, their keeper
   Was a cannie carefu' chiel'.

Ay when ony tentless lammie
   Wi' its neibours chanced to go,
Sandy kend the careless mammy,
   Whether she cried *mae* or no.

Warldly walth an' grandeur scornin',
   Peace adorned his little bield;
Ilka e'enin', ilka mornin',
   Sandy to his Maker kneeled.

You wha roun' wi' diamonds wrap ye,
   An' are fanned wi' loud applause,
Can ye trou the lad was happy?
   Really 'tis believed he was.

In the day sae black an' showery,
    I ha'e seen the bonny bow,
When arrayed in all its glory,
    Vanish on the mountain's brow.

Sae ha'e ye, my lovely marrow,
    Seen the rose an' vi'let blue,
Bloomin' on the banks of Yarrow,
    Quickly fade, an' lose their hue;

Fadin' as the forest roses,
    Transient as the radiant bow,
Fleetin' as the shower that follows,
    Is our happiness below.

Unadmired she'll hover near ye,
    In the rural sport she'll play;
Woo her—she'll at distance hear ye,
    Press her—she is gane for ay.

She had Sandy ay attendit,
    Seemed obedient to his nod;
Now his happy hours are endit,
    Lack-a-day for Sandy Tod!

I' the kirk ae Sunday sittin',
   Whar to be he seldom failed,
Sandy's tender heart was smitten
   Wi' a wound that never healed:

Sally, dressed i' hat an' feather,
   Placed her in a neibrin' pew,
Sandy sat—he kendna whether!
   Sandy felt—he wistna how!

Though the priest alarmed the audience,
   An' drew tears frae mony een,
Sandy heard a noise like baudrons
   Murrin' i' the bed at e'en!

Aince or twice his sin alarmed him,
   Down he looked, an' wished a prayer;
Sally had o' sense disarmed him,
   Heart an' mind an' a' was there!

Luckily her een were from him;
   Ay they beamed anither road;
Aince a smilin' glance set on him—
   " Mercy, Lord !" quo' Sandy Tod.

A' that night he lay an' turned him,
    Fastit a' the followin' day;
Now the eastern lamps war burnin',
    Westward fled the glomin' grey.

Res'lute made by desperation,
    Down the glen in haste he flew,
Quickly reached the habitation
    Where his sweet carnation grew.

I wad sing the happy meetin',
    War it new or strange to thee;
Weel ye ken 'tis but repeatin'
    What has past 'tween you and me.—

Thy white hand around me pressed,
    My unresty heart has felt;
But, whan hers on Sandy rested,
    His fond heart was like to melt!

Lockit to his bosom duntin'
    Listless a' the night she lay,
Orion's belt had bored the mountain,
    Loud the cock had crawed the day.

Sandy rase—his bonnet daddit—
 Begged a kiss—gat nine or ten;
Then the hay, sae ruffed an' saddit,
 Towzlet up that nane might ken.

You ha'e seen, on April mornin',
 Light o' heart, the pretty lamb
Skippin', dancin', bondage scornin',
 Wander heedless o' its dam?

Sometimes gaun, an' sometimes rinnin',
 Sandy to his mountains ran;
Roun' aboon his flocks gaed singin',
 Never was a blyther man:

Never did his native nation,
 Sun or sky, wear sic a hue;
In his een the hale creation
 Wore a face entirely new.

Weel he lo'ed his faithfu' Ruffler,
 Weel the bird sang on the tree;
Meanest creatures doomed to suffer,
 Brought the tear into his ee.

Sandy's heart was undesignin',
  Soft an' lovin' as the dove;
Scarcely cou'd it bear refinin'
  By the gentle fire o' love.

You ha'e seen the cunnin' fowler
  Wile the airy bird to death;
Blossoms nipt by breezes fouler,
  Or by winter's wastin' breath?

Sally's blossom soon was blighted
  By untimely winter prest;
Sally had been wooed an' slighted
  By a farmer in the west.

Sandy daily lo'ed her dearer,
  Kendna she afore was won,
Aince, whan he gaed down to see her,
  Sally had a dainty son!

Sternies, blush, an' hide your faces;
  Veil the moon in sable hue;
Else thy locks, for human vices,
  Soon will dreep wi' pity's dew!

Thou who rules the rolling thunder,
    Thou who darts the flying flame,
Wilt thou vengeance ay keep under
    Due for injured love an' fame!

Cease, my charmer, cease bewailin',
    Down thy cheeks the pearls shine;
Cease to mourn thy sex's failin',
    I maun drap a tear for mine:

Man, the lord o' the creation,
    Lightened wi' a ray divine,
Lost to feelin', truth, an' caution,
    Lags the brutal tribes behind!

You ha'e seen the harmless conie
    Following hame its mate to rest;
One ensnared, the frighted cronie
    Fled amazed wi' pantin' breast.

Petrified, an' dumb wi' horror,
    Sandy fled, he kendna where;
Never heart than his was sorer,
    It was mair than he cou'd bear!

Seven days on yonder mountain
   Lay he sobbin', late an' soon,
Till discovered by a fountain,
   Railin' at the dowy moon.

Weepin' a' the day, he'd wander
   Through yon dismal glen alane;
By the stream at night wad dander,
   Ravin' owr his Sally's name.

Shun'd an' pitied by the world,
   Long a humblin' sight was he,
Till that fatal moment hurled
   Him to lang eternity.

Sittin' on yon cliff sae rocky,
   Fearless as the boding crow,—
No, my dear, I winna shock ye
   Wi' the bloody scene below.

By yon aek, decayed an' rottin',
   Where the hardy woodbin twines,
Now, in peace, he sleeps forgotten;
   Owr his head these simple lines:—

" Lovers, pause, while I implore ye
   Still to walk in virtue's road;
An' to say, when ye gang o'er me,
   Lack a-day, for Sandy Tod!"

A FAREWELL TO ETTRICK.

Fareweel, my Ettrick! fare-ye-weel!
   I own I'm unco laith to leave ye;
Nane kens the half o' what I feel,
   Nor half the cause I ha'e to grieve me!

There first I saw the rising morn;
   There first my infant mind unfurl'd,
To judge that spot where I was born
   The very centre o' the world!

I thought the hills were sharp as knives,
   An' the braed lift lay whomel'd on them,
An' glowr'd wi' wonder at the wives
   That spak o' ither hills ayon' them.

When ilka year ga'e something new,
   Addition to my mind or stature,
As fast my love for Ettrick grew,
   Implanted in my very nature.

I've sung, in mony a rustic lay,
   Her heroes, an' her hills sae green;
Her woods and vallies fresh and gay;
   Her honest lads and lasses clean.

I had a thought—a poor vain thought!
   I thought that I might do her honour;
But a' my hopes are come to nought,
   I'm forc'd to turn my back upon her!

She's thrown me out o' house an' hauld!
   My heart got never sic a thrust!
An' my poor parents, frail an' auld,
   Are forc'd to leave their kindred dust!

But fare-ye-weel, my native streams
   Frae a' sic dule be ye preserv'd;
Ye'll find ye cherish some at hame
   That disna just sae weel deserve't.

There is nae man on a' your banks
    Will ever say that I did wrang him;
The lasses ha'e my dearest thanks
    For a' the joys I had amang them.

Though twin'd by rough an' ragin' seas,
    An' risin' hills an' rollin' rivers:
To think o' them I'll never cease,
    Until my heart ga'e a' to shivers!

I'll make the Harris rocks to ring
    Wi' ditties wild, when nane shall hear;
The Lewis shores shall learn to sing
    The names o' them I lo'ed so dear.

My Peggy's ay aboon the lave,
    I'll carve on ilka lonely green;
The sea-bird, tossin' on the wave,
    Shall learn the name o' bonny Jean.

Ye gods, tak care o' my dear lass!
    That as I leave her I may find her;
Till that blest time shall come to pass
    We'll meet again, and never sinder.

Fareweel, my Ettrick ! fare-ye-weel !
   I own I'm unco wae to leave ye !
Nane kens the half o' what I feel,
   Nor half o' that I ha'e to grieve me !

My parents, crazy grown wi' eild,
   How I rejoic'd to be their stay !
I thought to stand their help an' shield,
   Until an' at their latest day.

Wi' gentle hand to close their een,
   An' weet the yerd wi' mony a tear,
That held the dust o' ilka frien';
   O' friens so tender an' sincere !

It winna do:—I maun away
   To yon rough isle sae bleak an' dun ;
Lang will they mourn, baith night an' day,
   The absence o' their darlin' son.

An' my dear Will ! how will I fen'
   Without thy kind an' ardent care !
Without thy verse-inspirin' pen,
   My muse will sleep an' sing nae mair.

Fareweel to a' my kith an' kin!
   To ilka frien' I held sae dear!
How happy often hae we been,
   Wi' music, mirth, an' welcome cheer!

Nae mair your gilded banks at noon,
   An answer to my flute will swell!
Nae mair the viol sweet I'll tune,
   That a' the younkers lo'ed sae well!

Nae mair amang the bags an' rocks,
   While hounds wi' music fill'd the air,
We'll hunt the sly an' cruel fox,
   Or trace the warie, circlin' hare!

My happy days wi' you are past!
   An' waes my heart! will ne'er return!
The brightest day will overcast!
   And man was made at times to mourn.

But if I kend my dyin' day,
   Though distant, weary, pale, an' wan,
I'd tak my staff an' post away
   To yield my life where it began.

If in yon lone sequester'd place
   The tyrant Death should lay me low,
Oh! drap a tear, an' say—Alas!
   For him who lov'd an' honour'd you.

Fareweel, my Ettrick! fare-ye-weel!
   I own I'm something wae to leave ye!
Nane kens the half o' what I feel!
   Nor half the cause I ha'e to grieve me!

LOVE ABUSED.

Tune—*Mary, weep nae mair for me.*

The gloaming from the welkin high
   Had chased the bonny gouden gleam;
The curtained east, in crimson dye,
   Hung heavy o'er the tinted stream;
The wild rose, blushing on the brier,
   Was set with drops of shining dew—
As big, and clear, the bursting tear
   That rowed in Betty's een sae blue!

She saw the dear, the little cot,
   Where fifteen years flew sweetly bye!
And mourn'd her shame, and hapless lot,
   That forc'd her from that home to lie.

Though sweet and mild the evening smile,
    Her heart was rent with anguish keen;
The mavis ceased his music wild,
    And wonder'd what her sobs could mean.

" It was not kind, to rob my mind
    Of all its peace for evermore!
To blot my name with burning shame,
    And make my parents' hearts so sore.
That hame how dare I enter now,
    Each honoured face in tears to see,
Where oft I kneel'd, to hear the vow
    Was offer'd from the heart for me!

" And can I love the treacherous man
    Who wrought that dear and deadly ill,
Who blurr'd with clouds my early dawn?
    Ah! woes my heart! I love him still.
My heart abus'd, my love misus'd,
    My wretched fate with tears I see:
But most I fear, my parents dear
    Go mourning to the grave for me."

EPISTLE

TO

MR T. M. C., LONDON.

Published in the Scots Magazine.

───

My blessin' on you T. M. C.
Like you there are nae mony mae:
For mony a year, wi' eager een,
I've glowr'd owr Scotia's Magazine;
And oft, like zealots at a sermon,
Discoverin' beauties whar there were none;
But never a' my life, till now,
Have I met sic a chiel as you;
Sae sly, sae shrewd, sae queer a creature,
Sae weel acquaint wi' simple nature,
Sae gay, sae easy, an' sae ranty,
Sae cappernaity an' sae canty:
For when I sing your sangs sae gay,
To lasses at the bught or hay,

They blush, an' smurtlin', own they like them,
The thoughts they thought afore sae strike them.
　Whether 'tis from a similarity
Of feelings, hitting to a rarity;
Or if in verse you soar away,
Far, far beyond my simple lay,
An' into nature tak a stretch,
Whilk I wad fain, but canna reach;
Or if ae planet held the sway
When we were born, I canna say;
But frae sic causes, or some other,
I feel a wish to ca' you brother.
　Then, billy, set your foot to mine,
Let baith our buoyant brains combine
To raise our country's Magazine
Aboon the times that yet ha'e been.
Then tak some pains to double rhyme,
Gar line wi' line keep equal time,
An' then, though critics back should fling us,
The deils shall dadd in vain to ding us.

Though Pegasus may be denied,
By lofty bards sae occupied,
Wi' joy we'll mount our cuddy asses,
An' scour like fire around Parnassus,
An' gather flowers of ilka hue,
To bind auld Scotland's honest brow.
The upstarts new shall a' be snubbit,
And Ruddiman be sadly rubbit.

How could ye leave our hoary hills?
Our ruggit rocks and rattling rills?
Our woodlands wild, an' waters mony?
Our lasses chaste, an' sweet, an' bonny?
The warrior's nurse, the poet's theme!
The seat of innocence an'—hame?

We've sic a short time here to fare,
'Tis little matter how or where;
An' I wad chuse at least eleven
'Fore London, for the road to heaven.

I neither ken your name nor bearin'; *
Only I ken ye are a queer ane,

---

* The gentleman, to whom this epistle was addressed, is Mr Thomas Mouncey Cunninghame, from Dumfries-shire, the author of many ingenious essays in the Scots Magazine; but, at the writing of this, the author knew nothing of him.

An' guess, for insight, wealth, or knowledge,
Ye've ta'en the desk, or musty college;
To turn a pedant or translator,
And slight the genuine school of nature.
Sweet dame! she met me single handed;
Yet, studying her, my mind expanded
To bounds are neither rack'd nor narrow,
On Ettrick banks an' braes of Yarrow.

An' though your life should glide away
In pleasure's dear an' devious way,
Regret will sometimes pierce the heart,
An' leave a dour an' deadly smart.
An' when death comes, I'm wae for thee!
Nae real friend to close your ee!
Or owr a son or brother's bier
To shed the sad regretfu' tear!
But just let down, wi' strings an' pullies,
To sleep wi' w————es, an' bucks, an' bullies:
An' when the summons reach the dead anes,
To rise in droves frae 'mang the headstanes,
Poor Tam may gang an' stand alane,
Of fellow faces he'll see nane,
But a' the croud gaun throu'ther, throu'ther,
Wi' ruefu' looks out owr ilk shouther.

O leave that lake of louns an' letchery,
Of folly, falsehood, tricks, and treachery;
Though oft a thriving place for low wits,
L—d, it's a dangerous hole for poets!

If life's a blessing—tween twa brothers,
The poor enjoy't as lang as others.
If health surpasses sumptuous fare,
Of that they ha'e their ample share.
What wad ye ha'e then? Dinna wrang us,
Come back an' live an' die amang us.
I lang to sing a sonnet wi' thee,
An' bonny Bessy sighs to see thee:
O! when she's sic a kind an' bonny ane,
Come—wed, an' turn a Cameronian.

While round our coast the ocean rows;
While on the Grampians heather grows;
While goud and gear the miser heaps up,
An' ill-will between cadgers keeps up;
While simple ease improves the feature,
An' best becomes the cheek o' nature;
As sterns the sky, and spots the leopard,—
Count on

  Your friend,

    THE ETTRICK SHEPHERD.

SCOTIA'S GLENS.

Tune—Lord Ballantine's delight.

'Mong Scotia's glens, and mountains blue,
Where Gallia's lilies never grew,
Where Roman eagles never flew,
  Nor Danish lion rallied;
Where skulks the roe in anxious fear,
Where roves the stately nimble deer—
There live the lads to freedom dear,
  By foreign yoke ne'er galled.

There woods grow wild on every hill,
There freemen wander at their will;
Sure Scotland will be Scotland still,
  While hearts so brave defend her:

Fear not, our sovereign liege, they cry,
We've flourished fair beneath thine eye;
For thee we'll fight, for thee we'll die,
 'Nor ought but life surrender.

Since thou hast watched our every need,
And taught our navies wide to spread,
The smallest hair from thy grey head
 No foreign foe shall sever.
Thy honoured age in peace to save,
The sternest host we'll dauntless brave;
Or stem the stoutest Indian wave,
 No heart nor hand shall waver.

Though nations join yon tyrant's arm,
While Scotland's noble blood runs warm,
Our good old man we'll guard from harm,
 Or fall in heaps around him.
Although the Irish harp were won,
And England's roses all o'er-run,
'Mong Scotia's glens, wi' sword and gun,
 We'll form a bulwark round him.

DONALD MACDONALD.

Tune—Woo'd and married an' a'.

My name it is Donald Macdonald,
  I live in the Highlands sae grand;
I've followed our banner, an' will do,
  Wharever my maker has land.
When rankit amang the blue bonnets,
  Nae danger can fear me awa,
I ken that my brethren around me
  Are either to conquer or fa.'—
    Brogs an' brochen an' a',
    Brochen an' brogs an' a',
    An' isna the laddie weel aff
    Wha has brogs an' brochen an' a'.

Short syne we war wonderfu' canty,
  Our friends an' our country to see,
But since the proud Consul's grown vaunty,
  We'll meet him by land or by sea.
Wherever a clan is disloyal,
  Wherever our king has a foe,
He'll quickly see Donald Macdonald
  Wi' his Highlanders all in a row.—
    Guns an' pistols an' a',
    Pistols an' guns an' a';
    He'll quickly see Donald Macdonald
    Wi' guns an' pistols an' a'.

What though we befriendit young Charlie?
  To tell it I dinna think shame;
Poor lad! he came to us but barely,
  An' reckoned our mountains his hame:
'Tis true that our reason forbade us,
  But tenderness carried the day;
Had Geordie come friendless amang us,
  Wi' him we had a' gane away.—
    Sword an' buckler an' a',
    Buckler an' sword an' a';
    For George we'll encounter the devil,
    Wi' sword an' buckler an' a'.

An' O I wad eagerly press him
   The keys o' the East to retain;
For shou'd he gi'e up the possession,
   We'll soon ha'e to force them again;
Than yield up an inch wi' dishonour,
   Though it war my finishin' blow,
He ay may depend on Macdonald,
   Wi's Highlandmen all in a row.—
      Knees an' elbows an' a',
      Elbows an' knees an' a';
      Depend upon Donald Macdonald,
      His knees an' elbows an' a'.

If Bonapart land at Fort-William,
   Auld Europe nae langer shall grane;
I laugh, whan I think how we'll gall him
   Wi' bullet, wi' steel, an' wi' stane;
Wi' rocks o' the Nevis an' Gairy,
   We'll rattle him aff frae our shore;
Or lull him asleep in a cairney,
   An' sing him—*Lochaber no more!*
      Stanes an' bullets an' a',
      Bullets an' stanes an' a';
      We'll finish the Corsican callan',
      Wi' stanes an' bullets an' a'.

The Gordon is gude in a hurry;
 An' Campbell is steel to the bane;
An' Grant, an' Mackenzie, an' Murray,
 An' Cameron will hurkle to nane.
The Stuart is sturdy an' wannle,
 An' sae is Macleod an' Mackay;
An' I, their gude-brither Macdonald,
 Sal never be last i' the fray.
  Brogs an' brochen an' a',
  Brochen an' brogs an' a';
  An' up wi' the bonny blue bonnet,
  The kilt, an' the feather, an a'.

THE
AUTHOR'S ADDRESS
TO
HIS AULD DOG HECTOR.

Come, my auld, towzy, trusty friend;
   What gars ye look sae douth an' wae?
D'ye think my favour's at an end,
   Because thy head is turnin gray?

Although thy feet begin to fail,
   Their best were spent in serving me;
An' can I grudge thy wee bit meal,
   Some comfort in thy age to gi'e?

For mony a day, frae sun to sun,
   We've toil'd an' helpit ane anither;
An' mony a thousand mile thou'st run,
   To keep my thraward flocks thegither.

To nae thrawn boy, nor scrawghin wife,
   Shall thy auld banes become a drudge;
At cats an' callans, a' thy life,
   Thou ever bore a mortal grudge.

An' whiles thy surly looks declared,
   Thou lo'ed the women warst of a';
'Cause aft they my affection shared,
   Which thou couldst never bruik ata'.

When sitting with my bonny Meg,
   Mair happy than a prince could be,
Thou plac'd thee by her other leg,
   An' watched her wi' a jealous ee.

An' then, at ony start or steer,
   Thou wad ha'e worried furiouslye;
While I was forc'd to curse and swear,
   Afore thou wad forbidden be.

Yet wad she clasp thy towzy paw;
   Thy greesome grips were never skaithly;
An' thou than her hast been mair true!
   An' truer than the friend that ga'e thee!

Ah, me! of fashion, health, an' pride,
   The world has read me sic a lecture!
But yet it's a' in part repaid
   By thee, my faithful, grateful Hector!

O'er past imprudence, oft alane
   I've shed the saut an' silent tear;
Then, sharing ay my grief an' pain,
   My poor auld friend came snoovin' near.

For a' the days we've sojourned here,
   An' they've been neither fine nor few,
That thought possest thee year to year,
   That a' my griefs arase frae you.

Wi' waesome face, and hingin' head,
   Thou wad ha'e press'd thee to my knee;
While I thy looks as weel could read,
   As thou hadst said in words to me,—

" O my dear master, dinna greet;
   What ha'e I ever done to vex ye?
See here I'm cowrin' at your feet;
   Just take my life if I perplex ye.

" For a' my toil, my wee drap meat
    Is a' the wage I ask of thee;
For whilk I'm oft oblig'd to wait
    Wi' hungry wame, an' patient ee.

" Whatever wayward course ye steer;
    Whatever sad mischance o'ertake ye;
Man, here is ane will hald ye dear!
    Man, here's a friend will ne'er forsake ye!"

Yes, my puir beast! though friends me scorn,
    Whom mair than life I valued dear;
An' throw me out to fight forlorn,
    Wi' ills my heart dow hardly bear;

While I have thee to bear a part—
    My plaid; my health, an' heezle rung—
I'll scorn the silly haughty heart,
    The saucy look, and slanderous tongue.

Sure friends by pop'lar envy sway'd,
    Are ten times waur than ony fae!
My heart was theirs, an' to them laid
    As open as the light o' day.

I fear'd my ain; but never dredd
   That I for loss o' theirs should mourn;
Or that, when luck or favour fled,
   Their friendship wad injurious turn.

But He, who feeds the ravens young,
   Lets naething pass unheeded bye;
He'll sometime judge of right an' wrong,
   An' ay provide for you and I.

And hear me, Hector: thee I'll trust,
   As far as thou hast wit an' skill;
Sae will I ae sweet lovely breast,
   To me a balm for every ill.

To these my faith shall ever run,
   While I have reason truth to scan;
But ne'er, beyond my mother's son,
   To aught that bears the shape of man.—

I ne'er could thole thy cravin' face,
   Nor when ye pattit on my knee;
Though in a far an' unco place,
   I've whiles been forc'd to beg for thee.

Even now I'm in my master's power,
  Where my regard may scarce be shown;
But ere I'm forc'd to gi'e thee o'er,
  When thou art auld an' useless grown,

I'll get a cottage o' my ain,
  Some wee bit cannie, lonely biel',
Where thy auld heart shall rest fu' fain,
  An' share with me my humble meal.

Thy post shall be to guard the door,
  An' bark at pethers, boys, an' whips;
Of cats an' hens to clear the floor,
  An' bite the flaes that vex thy hips.

When my last bannock's on the hearth,
  Of that thou sanna want thy share;
While I have house or hald on earth,
  My Hector shall ha'e shelter there.

An' should grim death thy noddle save,
  Till he has made an end of me;
Ye'll lye a wee while on the grave
  Of ane wha ay was kind to thee.

There's nane alive will miss me mair;
  An' though in words thou canst not wail,
On a' the claes thy master ware,
  Thou'lt smell, and fawn, an' wag thy tail.

An' if I'm forc'd with thee to part,
  Which will be sair against my will,
I'll sometimes mind thy honest heart,
  As lang as I can climb a hill.

Come, my auld, touzy, trusty tike,
  Let's speel to Queensb'ry's lofty brow;
There greedy midges never fike;
  There care an' envy never grow.

While gazing down the fertile dales,
  Content an' peace shall ay be by;
An' muses leave their native vales
  To rove at large wi' you and I.

THE BONNETS O' BONNY DUNDEE.

Tune.—*Comin' thro' the Rye.*

"O will ye gang down to the bush in the meadow,
 An' see how the ewes an' the lammies do feed O!
An' by the fair hand, thro' the flowers I will lead you,
 An' sing you the bonnets o' bonny Dundee."
"Wi' heart an' wi' hand, my dear lad! I'll gang wi' thee;
 My daddy an' mammy think nought to belie thee;
I ken ye'll do naething but kiss me, an' lead me,
 An' sing me the bonnets o' bonny Dundee."

O! when fled thy angel, poor lovely Macmillan!
   An' left thee to listen to counsel sae killin';
O where were the feelings o' that smiling villain,
   Wha riffled thy blossom, an' left thee to die?
How pale is that cheek that was rosy an' reid, O!
   To see that sunk eye wad gar ony heart bleed, O;
O wae to the wild-willow bush in the meadow;
   O dool to the bonnets o' bonny Dundee!

AULD ETTRICK JOHN.

There dwalt a man on Ettrick side,
    An' onest man I wot was he;
His name was John, an' he was born
    A year afore the thretty three:
He wad a wife when he was young,
    But she had deit, an' John was wae;
He wantit lang, at length did gang,
    To court the lassie o' the brae.

Auld John cam daddin down the hill,
    His arm was waggin manfullie;
He thought his shadow look'd na ill,
    As aft he keek'd aside to see.

His shoon war four pound weight a-piece;
   On ilka leg a ho had he;
His doublet strang was large an' lang,
   His breeks they hardly reach'd his knee.

His coat was threed-about wi' green,
   The mouds* had wrought it muckle harm;
The pouches war an ell atween,
   The cuff was faldit up the arm.
He wore a bonnet on his head,
   The bung upon his shoulders lay,
An' by the neb ye wad hae red,
   That Johnie view'd the milky way.

But yet for a' his antic dress,
   His cheeks wi' healthy red did glow;
His joints war knit, an firm like brass,
   Though siller gray his head did grow:
An' John, altho' he had nae lands,
   Had twa gude kye among the knowes;
A hunder pund i' honest hands,
   An' sax an' thretty doddit yowes.

                * Mouds, *moths.*

An' Nelly was a bonny lass,
    Fu' sweet an' ruddy was her mow',
Her een war like twa beads o' glass;
    Her brow was white like Cheviot woo.
Her cheeks war bright as heather bells,
    Her bosom like December snaw,
Her teeth as pure as eggs's shells,
    Her hair was like the hoddy craw.

' Gude wife," quo John, as he sat down,
    " I'm come to court your daughter Nell;
An' if I die immediately,
    She sall hae a' the gear hersell.
An' if I chance to hae a son,
    I'll breed him up a bra divine;
An' if ilk wiss turn out a we'an,
    There's little fear that we hae nine."

Now Nelly thought, an' ay she leugh,
    " Our lads are a' for sodgers gane;
Young Tam will kiss an' toy enough,
    But he o' marriage talketh nane.

When I am laid in Johnnie's bed,
  Like hares or lav'rocks I'll be free;
I'll busk me braw an' conquer a',
  Auld Johnnie's just the man for me."

Wi' little say he wan the day,
  She soon becam his bonny bride;
But ilka joy is fled away,
  Frae Johnie's canty ingle side;
She frets an' greets, an' visits aft,
  In hopes some lad will see her hame;
But never ane will be sae daft,
  As tent auld Johnie's flisky dame.

An' John will be a gaishen soon;
  His teeth are frae their sockets flown,
The hair's peel'd aff his head aboon,
  His face is milk an' water grown:
His legs, that firm like pillars stood,
  Are now grown toom an' unco sma';
She's reav'd him sair o' flesh an' blood,
  An peace o' mind,—the warst ava.

Let ilka lassie tak a man,
　An' ilka callan tak a wife;
But youth wi' youth, gae hand in hand,
　Or tine the sweetest joys o' life.
Ye men whae's heads are turnin' gray,
　Wha to the grave are hastin' on,
Let reason ay your passion sway,
　An' mind the fate o' Ettrick John.

An' a' ye lasses plump an' fair,
　Let pure affection guide your hand,
Nor stoop to lead a life o' care,
　Wi' wither'd age, for gear or land.
When ilka lad your beauty slights,
　An' ilka smile shall yield to wae,
Ye'll mind the lang an' lanesome nights
　O' Nell, the lassie o' the brae.

THE HAY MAKING.

Tune.—*Comin' thro' the Rye.*

O Tibby, lassie, how I loe,
  'Tis needless here to tell;
But a' the flowers the meadow through,
  Ye're sweetest ay yoursel!
I canna sleep a wink at night,
  Nor work i' peace by day;
Your image smiles afore my sight,
  Whate'er I do or say.

Fy, Jamie, dinna act the part
  Ye'll ever blush to own,
Nor try to draw my youthfu' heart
  Frae reason's sober throne.

Sic visions I can ne'er approve,
    Nor ony waukin' dream;
Than hae sic fiery furious love,
    I'd rather hae esteem.

My bonnie lassie, come away,
    I canna bide your frown;
Wi' ilka flower sae fresh an' gay,
    I'll deck your bosom roun'.
I'll pu' the gowan off the glen,
    The lillie off the lee,
The rose an' hawthorn sweet I'll twine,
    To make a bobb for thee.

Aye, Jamie, ye wad steal my heart,
    An' a my peace frae me,
An' hank me fast within the net,
    Ere I my error see.
Ye'll pu' the gowan off the glen,
    My bosom to adorn,
An' ye confess ye're gaun to place
    Within my breast a thorn!

How can ye, Tibby, be so tart,
　　An' vex me a' the day?
Ye ken I loe wi' a' my heart,
　　What wad ye hae me say?
Ilk anxious wish, an' little care,
　　I'll in thy breast confide;
An' a' your joys an' sorrows share,
　　If ye'll become my bride.

Then tak my hand, ye hae my heart,
　　There's nane I like sae weel,
And Heaven grant I act my part
　　To ane sae true and leel.
An' we'll win' the hay, an wear the hay,
　　Till death our bosoms twine,
An' often bless the happy day,
　　That join'd us lang syne.

BONNY JEAN.

Tune—Prince William Henry's Delight.

Sing on, sing on, my bonny bird,
   The sang ye sang yestreen O,
When here, aneath the hawthorn wild,
   I met my bonny Jean O.
My blude ran prinklin' through my veins,
   My hair began to steer O;
My heart play'd deep against my breast!
   As I beheld my dear O.

O weels me on my happy lot!
   O weels me on my dearie!
O weels me on the charmin' spot,
   Where a' combin'd to chear me!

201

The mavis liltit on the bush,
    The lavrock on the green O,
The lilie bloom'd, the daisy blush'd,
    But a' was nought to Jean O.

Sing on, sing on, my bonnie thrush,
    Be neither flee'd nor eerie,
I'll wad your love sits i' the bush,
    That gars ye sing sae cheerie;
She may be kind, she may be sweet,
    She may be neat an' clean O;
But O she's e'en a drysome mate,
    Compar'd wi' bonny Jean O.

If love wad open a' her stores,
    An' a' her bloomin' treasures,
An' bid me rise an' turn an' choice,
    An' taste her chiefest pleasures;
My choice wad be the rosy cheek,
    The modest beamin' eye, O!
The yellow hair, the bosom fair,
    The lips o' coral dye, O!

A bramble shade around our head,
    A burnie poplin' bye, O,
Our bed the swaird, our sheet the plaid,
    Our canopy the sky O!
An' here's the burn, an' there's the bush
    Around the flowrie green O;
An' this the plaid, an' sure the lass
    Wad be my bonnie Jean O.

Hear me, thou bonny modest moon!
    Ye sternies twinklin' high O!
An' a' ye gentle powers aboon,
    That roam athwart the sky O.
Ye see me gratefu' for the past,
    Ye saw me blest yestreen O;
An' ever till I breathe my last,
    Ye'll see me true to Jean O.

FINIS.

www.ingramcontent.com/pod-product-compliance
Lightning Source LLC
LaVergne TN
LVHW061308060426
835507LV00019B/2063